A History of the Great Western Railway
3. Wartime and the Final Years, 1939–48

Also available from Allen and Unwin

GREAT WESTERN SAINTS & SINNERS by W. A. Tuplin
GREAT WESTERN STEAM by W. A. Tuplin
MEN OF THE GREAT WESTERN by Peter Grafton
SOUTH WEST RAILWAYMAN by Donald King
GRAVEYARD OF STEAM by Brian Hindley
GREAT CENTRAL STEAM by W. A. Tuplin
HISTORY OF THE LMS vols 1–3 by O. S. Nock
HISTORY OF THE LNER vols 1–3 by Michael R. Bonavia
RAILS TO DISASTER by Malcolm Gerard and J. A. B. Hamilton
LONDON MIDLAND MAINLINE CAMERAMAN by W. Philip Conolly
MAUNSELL'S NELSONS by D. W. Winkworth
MEN OF THE LNER by Peter Grafton
ON AND OFF THE RAILS by Sir John Elliot
PRESERVED STEAM IN BRITAIN by Patrick B. Whitehouse
RIDDLES STANDARD TYPES IN TRAFFIC by G. Freeman Allen
THE SCHOOLS 4–4–0S by D. W. Winkworth
STEAM'S INDIAN SUMMER by George Heiron and Eric Treacy
TRAINS OF THOUGHT ed. A. W. Hobson
TRAINS TO NOWHERE by J. A. B. Hamilton
TRAVELLING BY TRAIN IN THE EDWARDIAN AGE by Philip Unwin

A History of the Great Western Railway
3. Wartime and the Final Years, 1939-48

Peter Semmens, M.A., C.Chem., F.R.S.C., M.B.C.S., M.C.I.T.

GUILD PUBLISHING
LONDON

This edition published 1985 by Book Club Associates by arrangement with
George Allen & Unwin

Second impression 1986
Third impression 1987

Picture research by Mike Esau

Set in 10 on 12 point Bembo by Nene Phototypesetters Ltd, Northampton
and printed and bound in Great Britain by
Biddles Ltd, Guildford and King's Lynn

Contents

List of Illustrations and Tables   *page*   9
1   World War II   11
2   The Final Years   60
3   Nationalisation   81
4   The Tradition Lives On   85
5   God's Wonderful Railway   93
     Index   97

List of Illustrations and Tables

1	1939 Railway Executive Poster	*page*	13
2	GWR excursion coaches as wartime office accommodation		15
3	Restaurant car with blackout curtains		18
4	After the air raid at Newton Abbot 1940		21
5	Train damaged by bombs at Bristol Temple Meads		23
6	Dean goods locomotive no. 156 ready for war service		27
7	USA 2–8–0 no. 2339 at Reading West Junction		30
8	The first Modified Hall class no. 6959		34
9	A streamlined railcar under construction at Swindon		35
10	Sherman tanks in Acton yard, 1942		37
11	George Allison giving a talk to GWR staff		40
12	Steel cases for 1000 lb bombs being made at Swindon		41
13	Broccoli being unloaded at Paddington		42
14	Maidenhead station in July 1941		45
15	The 'girl announcer' at Paddington		45
16	Crowds at Paddington in July 1942		48
17	The day Paddington station closed		51
18	The SS 'St Julian' as a hospital ship		51
19	Wartime activity at Cardiff Docks		53
20	GWR road vehicles at Paddington		55
21	A GWR mobile fire-fighting train and crew		56
22	Castle class no. 5071 'Spitfire'		58
23	No. 1020 'County of Monmouth' with single chimney		61
24	'Garth Hall' fitted for oil burning		63
25	Gas Turbine no. 18000 outside the test plant in Vienna		64
26	Exterior of a Hawksworth brake composite coach		68

27	Interior of a 3rd class Hawksworth coach	*page*	69
28	1st class salon of a refurbished GWR restaurant car		71
29	Castle class no. 5056 on an ATC test train		73
30	Work on the western extension of the LPTB Central line		74
31 32	} Reorganisation of goods traffic arrangements in 1946		76–7
33	The SS 'St Patrick' at Weymouth		79
34	Hall class arriving at Marylebone during the 1948 Exchanges		82
35	Castle class 4–6–0 on a train of Southern stock		83
36	Pannier tank and GWR semaphore signals near Cheltenham		86
37	Diesel-hydraulic no. D 1000 leaving High Wycombe		89
38	'City of Truro' at Newbury on a Southampton train		90
39	Pannier tank taking water at Drinnick Mill		91
40	Viscount Portal on the footplate of 'Garth Hall'		94

Tables

1	Timekeeping of Weekday GWR Passenger Trains – Winter 1939/40	*page*	32
2	Timekeeping of Weekday GWR Passenger Trains – 1938/45		33
3	GWR Passenger Traffic – Originating Journeys		36
4	Great Western Freight Traffic		39
5	Imports and Exports at the GW's South Wales Ports		44
6	Visitors at GW Hotels		52
7	Great Western Net Revenue – 1939/47		76
8	GWR's Interest and Dividends from Investments – 1947		78
9	Railway Dividends		79
10	Assets of the GWR Vested in British Transport Commission – 1948		81
11	Exchange Rates for 3% British Transport Stock		83
12	Exchange Rates and Yields on Ordinary Shares		84

I

World War II

When the Nazi invasion of Poland caused Britain and France to declare war on Germany in September 1939, the six subsequent years of hostilities were to involve the Great Western Railway directly in the conflict to an unprecedented extent. Although in Volume Two our narrative broke off at the outbreak of war, its coming had cast long shadows before. So far as the railways of this country were concerned, much preparatory work had taken place over the previous years since the setting up of the Railway Technical Committee in 1937 and reflected the same approach that was taking place generally in the larger sections of British industry.

In our account of the war years it is often difficult to disentangle the Great Western's activities from those of the railways of Britain generally, because, as in World War I, they were all operated by a single body on behalf of the Government. This was the Railway Executive Committee, first called into being in September 1938 but not given formal powers until the signing of the Emergency (Railway Control) order on 1 September 1939. The Great Western's General Manager, Sir James Milne, was their representative on this body, whose headquarters were in the closed Down Street station on the London Passenger Transport Board Piccadilly Line, deep underground. He was also the chair-

man of the railways' General Managers' Conference, an office he held for a number of years, but it was his position on the Railway Executive Committee that was to produce a somewhat unusual situation. In recognition of his long and distinguished service as their own General Manager, the Great Western elected him a director of the company in the autumn of 1940. However, since the Railway Executive Committee was a government body, those serving on it were not able to hold directorships of companies, and Sir James' position on the GWR board became a case of suspended animation, although his influence, advice and authority could hardly have suffered.

Air Raid Precautions and The Blitz

In World War I the railways of Britain had become involved in extensive movements of troops and munitions, and the same thing happened in the second conflict two decades later. The big difference in World War II, however, was that the development of aerial warfare brought the railways of Britain under attack on a scale that was only matched by the quantities of fire and high-explosive bombs that rained down on cities, docks and factories. Although the Spanish Civil War had given a preview of what might be expected, the widespread nature of the Blitz was not foreseen. Indeed the Great Western produced two posters, the second featured in their *Magazine* as late as 1940, which proclaimed 'The West is Best' – put your factory there NOW'. Amongst the places indicated on the map were Plymouth, Bristol and the South Wales ports, all of which were to suffer great devastation from night bombing raids. It is interesting to speculate how our modern advertising standards legislation would cope with such a situation.

The Great Western, like the other railway companies, had, even by 1939, undertaken much in the way of Air Raid Precautions (ARP), helped by a government grant of £4 million at the end of 1938. They were expected, as employers, to add a further £1¼m or so from their own resources. The allocation of the total between the different companies was not entirely based on their relative sizes, as the Great Western only received £472,000 of government money for its direct use, whereas the Southern's share was nearly £497,000 and the LMS's £1.36 million. This money was not spent only on measures to save lives during and after a raid, but to ensure that the railways were able to deal with any interruptions caused by bombing as rapidly as possible. As we will see later, considerable new works were undertaken during the war on the GWR, as elsewhere, in order to provide alternative routes for use in an emergency, or to handle the new traffic flows that developed as the country moved from defence to attack. The Great Western was also involved in the distribution of the materials for the Anderson shelters provided for the most vulnerable areas in the country. The initial government order for 400,000 of these was placed in 1939 and involved some 180,000 tons of steel, much of it consisting of specially-shaped corrugated sheeting. Many different manufacturers were involved and two-thirds of the sheet sections were produced in the Great Western's territory. The arrival of the twenty different major components, plus the bag of accessories, had to be coordinated by the railways, who then distributed sets of parts to the houses concerned. By May 1939 the GWR alone was distributing parts for 6,000 shelters each week from eight different stations, and the process continued elsewhere.

As far as ARP training was concerned, the work was in full swing well before the government grants were made available. The June 1938 issue of the *Great Western Railway Magazine* carried a long article on staff training arrangements, which was illustrated by a photograph of a practical demonstration at Paddington. A group of dark-suited railway officers, twenty-five strong, all wearing gas masks, stood on some pointwork alongside the main line, watching one of the party smothering a simulated incendiary bomb with sand. In the background the driver and fireman of a passing 'Star' leant from the cab to see what was going on. At that time eight ARP training schools were already in operation or planned throughout the railway.

Another very significant feature of the Home Front in World War II was the blackout. In theory no lighting installation was to show any beam upwards, and out in the open the ground was not to be illuminated sufficiently to be visible from the air any appreciable distance away. Domestic and office windows were relatively easy to deal with, but railway installations were a major headache. Major stations, such as Paddington, had acres of glass roofing, all of which had to be replaced with solid material for black-out purposes, although there was also a vital need to remove the potential dangers of the glass falling on those below after being shattered by the blast from a nearby bomb. Even after these modifications it was not possible to use ordinary levels of lighting, and

NOTICE
TO RAILWAY PASSENGERS

NOTICE IS HEREBY GIVEN

that, due to the National Emergency, the following alterations in Passenger Train travel, as applying to the Railways in Great Britain, will come into force on and from **MONDAY, 11th SEPTEMBER, 1939**:-

1. **Passenger Train Services.**
   The Passenger Train Services will be considerably curtailed and decelerated. For details see the Company's Notices.

2. **Cancellation of Reduced Fare Facilities.**
   Excursion and Reduced Fare facilities (except Monthly Return, Week-end, and Workmen's tickets) will be discontinued until further notice.

3. **Season and Traders' Tickets.**
   Season and Traders' tickets will continue to be issued.

4. **Reservation of Seats, Compartments, Etc.**
   The reservation of seats and compartments, and saloons for private parties will be discontinued.

5. **Restaurant Cars and Sleeping Cars.**
   Restaurant Car facilities will be withdrawn, and only a very limited number of Sleeping Cars will be available.

By Order
11th September, 1939.   THE RAILWAY EXECUTIVE COMMITTEE.

1. Poster issued by the Railway Executive Committee on September 11th 1939 putting the railways of Britain on a wartime footing.

dim blue bulbs became commonplace, while platform edges were whitened.

Elsewhere there were many open-air railway installations where lighting was vital if operations were to continue through the hours of darkness. While the ordinary levels of illumination in the 1930s were not up to those that are taken for granted today, or required by the Health and Safety at Work Regulations, they were still more than could be permitted under blackout conditions. The Great Western was involved in a large-scale blackout experiment in January 1939, in conjunction with the local authorities. As far as the railway was concerned, the trials involved Paddington station and offices as well as the line as far as Old Oak Common. A train equipped with the Home Office's approved levels of screened lighting was run down the line so that an official inspection could be made of the effectiveness of the precautions. In practice it was discovered that the permitted lighting levels were too low to allow railway operations to take place at night without hazard to the staff or delay to the operations.

Some months after hostilities had started, Acton Yard was used as an example to seek official relaxation of the current lighting standards. Although more wagons were being handled during the day shift, the throughput during the hours of darkness was down by a third. The night is traditionally the period when freight movements are at their heaviest, and it was not possible to utilise the spare day-time capacity, even by drafting in extra pannier tank locomotives to help with the shunting. Some relaxation in the lighting levels was permitted, but all such installations had to be equipped so that the lights could be turned off with a single switch in the event of an air raid. Although this involved the GWR having to rewire no less than 136 stations and yards, it provided the facility to give better levels of lighting for operational purposes, which could then rapidly be reduced if enemy aircraft approached. As the war continued and the detection of enemy aircraft was improved, it became possible to utilise this equipment to ease the problems of those working on the tracks in yards, although they were never permitted to be improved as much as the railways would have wished. Even as late as 1944, the publication *British Railways in Peace and War* still referred to the fact that the levels of outdoor lighting '. . . remain the most persistent drag on railway operation'.

Steam-hauled trains presented their own problems in the blackout. Today we are not accustomed to seeing steam specials operate at night, but Cuneo's 'Night King' painting provides a good example of the glare that emerged from the firehole door every time the fireman added a shovelful of coal. On stopping trains, the crews were taught only to fire in stations when the firebox was at its least incandescent, but this was not possible with an express train. Tarpaulin sheets were stretched between cab roof and tender to minimise the glare but made conditions on the footplate very bad indeed. On the GWR the side windows of their post-1923 cabs were sheeted over for the duration, while many of the tank locomotives already had, as standard, sliding metal shutters which could be used to cut down the emission of light. There were various stories during the war that trains had led enemy bombers to attack particular localities. Although none of my wartime flying was done at night with the ground below blacked out, I very much doubt that a heavy bomber could 'zero in' on the intermittent glow from the cab of a single moving locomotive a mile or more below. The situation was very different with daytime intruder raids with fighter-bombers as was practised so effectively by the RAF over Europe later in the war. Then the tell-tale plume of steam from a locomotive could provide a distant indication of the target which could be attacked at low level by a highly-manoeuvrable aircraft. This was one of the reasons which prompted the Germans to develop the use of condensing tenders for their locomotives operating on the Russian front. Static railway installations were, of course, only too prominent from the air, even at night, given any degree of moonlight, with their fans of tracks and the extensive roofs of large stations and goods depots.

The blackout also affected the lighting in railway carriages. Once the necessary arrangements had been worked out and applied, the usual arrangement was for a black strip about three inches wide to be applied round the edge of every compartment window. With the blinds pulled down, this gave an adequate light seal with the shaded overhead lights. Corner seats in consequence became far less popular for those wanting to read at night. The windows on corridors were not blacked out and only minimal levels of blue lighting were permitted. It was possible to relax these standards early in 1943 when the interiors of the light shades in the compartments of corridor stock were painted white, virtually doubling the level of lighting. At the same time white lights were permitted in the corridors in place of the blue ones. On non-corridor suburban stock the same relaxations were not allowed because of the greater frequency with which doors were opened at stations.

In spite of all these precautions, railway installations in this country, including those of the Great Western, were extensively hit by bombs during the war. In view of their vital importance for the war effort it was hardly surprising that they should be specifically singled out for attack, while in large cities subjected to indiscriminate bombing the extensive area covered by the stations and other railway installations inevitably resulted in their receiving a considerable weight of bombs. Paddington station had direct hits, and many other large stations on the Great Western were similarly damaged to a greater or lesser extent during the hostilities. One evening in August 1940 the station and locomotive depot at Newton Abbot were bombed and machine-

2. The GWR's attractively-styled excursion coaches were no strangers to Newbury Racecourse in pre-war days (see volume 2). With the outbreak of hostilities, however, some of the coaches were based there as office accommodation away from the threat of air raids. One of the staff in the far compartment sports his ARP badge on his lapel.

gunned by three enemy aircraft which arrived before the sirens had sounded. Four railway staff were killed, together with ten members of the public, and considerable damage was caused. Trackwork, the station buildings and rolling stock were badly damaged, the worst hit of the locomotives, pannier tank no 2785, being cut up on the spot afterwards, thus becoming one of the few British railway locomotives to be damaged beyond repair. One bomb failed to explode but, had it done so, the damage to no 6010 'King Charles I' would have been even more severe. As it was, a delay of ten hours occurred while the disposal squad was summoned and dealt with the bomb. Fortunately 'Tiny', the broad-gauge locomotive displayed on the down platform, was not damaged.

Bridges were particularly vulnerable, and great efforts were made to repair bomb damage in the minimum possible time. One bridge in South Wales received a direct hit from a high-explosive bomb in 1941 which blew thirty feet

15

of one of the abutments into the river. The main girders were bent while some of the permanent way and cross-girders were damaged beyond repair. Not only had the debris to be removed, but traffic had to be restored on the four adjacent lines, most of which were reopened next day. Sleeper cribs were built to support the damaged structure and the use of four new girders from stock enabled the two lines over the damaged span to be reopened, subject to a 25 mph speed restriction, three days later. Operations such as these reflected great credit on all involved, and it must be remembered that repairing the damage to the railway installations was usually only part of the aftermath of a raid, which, more often than not, left streets blocked with debris, while staff and their families also had to make good their own damage at home. Moreover, the presence of unexploded bombs could cause great inconvenience until they had been dealt with by the bomb disposal squads.

Much good work was carried out to restore the lines in this way, but Great Western railwaymen were involved in many heroic incidents in the immediate aftermath of raids. On an evening in October 1940, one of a stick of three bombs that landed in Praed Street, Paddington, outside the Great Western Royal Hotel, penetrated into the Inner Circle station below. The Great Western's ARP teams went into action immediately, with the Lawn becoming a casualty clearing station. All those seriously injured had been sent to hospital, some in commandeered vehicles, well within an hour of the bombs exploding. There were many more incidents in which the railway staff were at even greater personal risk. *The Great Western Railway Magazine* for January 1941 mentioned the names of ten members of staff who had shown '. . . courage and gallantry on the Great Western home front'. One of them was Acting Horse Foreman George Cooper who, with his three staff, saved thirty-six horses

and their stables after a raid, remaining on duty for forty-eight hours with only short rest periods. It was Shunter Norman Tunna's gallantry, however, that was marked by the award of the George Cross. After a raid at Birkenhead, he climbed on to a wagon containing 250lb high explosive bombs and prised them apart to remove the incendiary bomb which was jammed between them and burning furiously. Quite apart from the heat, the combination of magnesium and thermite was sufficient to burn its way through steel; but with his shunting pole Shunter Tunna was able to get rid of the bomb and then, with the assistance of the locomotive crew, cooled the load down with buckets of water until it was safe. He received his award from King George VI at an investiture at Buckingham Palace, which he attended in his uniform, accompanied by his wife and son. Prominent on his lapel was the badge issued to all railwaymen during the war, registering their service towards the war effort, since, in the main, those on the railways were in reserved occupations and not liable to be called up for military service.

Motive Power

In one of his early wartime speeches, Winston Churchill asked America to 'give us the tools and we will finish the job'. Similarly, during the hostilities, the railways needed new equipment and facilities to meet their wartime commitments. As far as locomotives were concerned, Swindon was not only involved in the construction of new ones for use at home, but also the adaptation of others for service overseas. The Great Western also borrowed considerable numbers of locomotives from the other three companies, as well as using some specially built for war service on both sides of the Atlantic.

At the beginning of the war, when the British Expeditionary Force was sent to France in the expectation that the war would be, in effect, a continuation of World War I, the Army required its own railway motive power behind the lines. Just before hostilities started the War Office was talking in terms of requiring no less than 800 locomotives in service overseas in the first twelve months of the war, which gives a clear indication of the extent to which the army relied on rail transport at that time.

From the Great Western's point of view, they were called on to provide some of those military stalwarts, the Dean Goods 0–6–0s. Sixty-two of these had been sent to France in 1917, of which sixteen were transferred to Salonika. Seven of these never came back although two were sold to the Ottoman Railway and continued at work there for many years. As we saw in the second part of this study, during the 1930s the Dean Goods were being replaced by the Collett 2251 class 0–6–0s, but at the outbreak of war in 1939 nine of the most recently withdrawn locomotives were promptly reinstated on the stock list. Many of these were amongst the hundred called up for military service. Before they left for France, however, considerable changes were required, most of which were carried out at Swindon, although fourteen were dealt with at Eastleigh. The ATC cab signalling equipment was removed and Westinghouse braking equipment provided instead of the normal GWR vacuum type. At least one locomotive acquired a Flaman speed recorder, its magnificent brass case no doubt requiring considerable attention afterwards from its military crews, although the locomotives themselves were painted in dull black with the letters W D, separated by a broad arrow, on the tender in pale yellow, like the army number on the cab side. Ten of them were specially fitted with condensing gear and pannier tanks, while equipment was also provided to enable them to lift water out of any convenient stream or pond to replenish their supplies.

After Dunkirk, when the Nazi forces had turned south to invade France, many of these 0–6–0s were captured and appreciable numbers of them were subsequently used by the SNCF, those allocated to the area served by the former Etat Railway even being renumbered in their series 030 WO 01 – 030 WO 045. After the end of the war, some locomotives that saw service in France were sent to China under United Nations' auspices, but many of the others were returned to England in 1948 and 1949 for scrapping amongst the rest of the war surplus material. They had been sold by the GWR to the War Department, so Swindon had no interest in them; in some cases they were actually cut up at Dover when they had arrived on the train ferry from France.

Many of these WD locomotives which had not been sent to France at the time of the German invasion also had an adventurous war. Initially they operated at various military establishments in this country, but some subsequently went abroad to North Africa and Italy. Certain of them even acquired names at different times in North Africa. 'Monty' and 'Wavell' were perhaps understandable, but the latter later became 'Margaret' while WD No 171 was first named 'Betty' and then 'Francis'. Clearly the policy that applied was well removed from the GWR's highly-organised class system.

To compensate for the loss of these 0–6–0s, the Great Western reinstated twenty of different classes that had been withdrawn but not cut up or sold, and borrowed forty 0–6–0s from the LMS and a similar number from the LNER. The former were class 2Fs and 3Fs of Midland Railway origin, and the latter J25s of NER vintage.

In World War I considerable numbers of

3. From October 16th 1939 restaurant car services were reintroduced on the GWR after light-proof blackout curtains had been fitted.

2–8–0s had been constructed by the War Department for military use. They were of Robinson's Great Central design, and some of them were still at work on the GWR in 1939, having been purchased by them after the war. About 300 of 'these locomotives, still in service throughout the country, were expected to have been requisitioned for war service in 1939, but the immediate need did not arise and they remained at work with their owning companies. These Robinson locomotives were only intended as a stop gap, as in 1939 the War Department had ordered 240 new 2–8–0s from various private manufacturers. These were of Stanier's 8F design for the LMS, introduced in 1935, which made them the most modern class of that wheel arrangement, and so were a logical choice. The first locomotives were completed in 1940 and many of them received LMS running numbers. The majority of them were then lent to the Great Western which put them to work on heavy freights, to help meet their shortage of motive power, which was further supplemented by the loan of 30 LNER class O4 2–8–0s until early 1943. After a much briefer spell of use on the GWR, most of the LMS locomotives were shipped abroad to the Middle East where they were used extensively as far afield as Iran, Turkey and Egypt. After the Allied invasion of Italy some operated there as well. The batch for Iran was altered for oil firing and Swindon was involved in the programme of conversion work along with the Southern and LMS. When the war was over, some of these locomotives returned to England and were taken into LMS stock, but others remained in the Middle East for the remainder of their working lives, which in Turkey extended into the 1980s. Two on the Egyptian State Railways were emblazoned with the title 'The Orient Express' on the cab sheets after the war, being used on the Cairo – Haifa express.

The Stanier 2–8–0s on loan to GWR in the early years of the war were not to be that railway's only involvement with that particular class of LMS locomotive, as Swindon subsequently built eighty for their own use, while others were constructed by the Southern and LNER. This move resulted from a Ministry of War Transport directive laying down that future wartime construction of 2–8–0s should be to a standard design which would, if necessary, also be suitable for military service overseas.

The locomotives borrowed from the Southern in the early 1940s were a somewhat more mixed bag, and comprised ten 4–6–0s, two 4–4–2Ts and a pair of dock shunters which were almost immediately passed on to the Admiralty.

Fine though the Crewe 2–8–0s were in their wartime version with various improvements such as thicker frames, they nevertheless represented a de luxe design by the middle of the war, and it was decided that a new class would be built instead for War Department use from 1943 onwards. A total of 935 of these 2–8–0 locomo-

tives was constructed, having been designed by Riddles and known as 'Austerities' because of their appearance. They were shipped to Europe after D-day, but 450 were initially lent to the LMS, LNER and Southern for use in this country. The Great Western was left out at first because they were extensively involved in receiving and commissioning the American Class S160 2–8–0s, as will be described later. The latter, however, were recalled in late 1944, ready to follow up the American armies after the start of the Second Front, and eighty-nine of the British 'Austerities' were transferred to the GWR by way of replacement, before they too crossed the Channel on the specially-equipped SR train ferries. Swindon's involvement with the Riddles design at this stage was short-lived but when hostilities ended they played a large part in overhauling the returned locomotives for permanent use on our railway system.

The American 2–8–0 locomotives were produced by a design team involving the US Army Corps of Transportation and the three largest locomotive manufacturers in that country, Alco, Baldwin and Lima. They were built to the standard British loading gauge so they could operate fairly widely in this country before moving on to the mainland of Europe, where clearances, although more generous than our own, were rather less than those in North America. As a result the S160s did not dwarf the British locomotives alongside which they were to work for some time. At first sight there was a considerable similarity between them and the Riddles 'Austerity' 2–8–0s, both having, by ordinary British standards, insignificant chimneys perched on large parallel smokeboxes. Both looked very strange to those of us used to the classic lines of Great Western locomotives. On close inspection there were numerous differences between the two 2–8–0 classes, and once one started to compare engineering details, the different design traditions on the two sides of the Atlantic became very apparent.

The Great Western was host to the first of the United States locomotives to enter service formally, when it was handed over at a ceremony at Paddington on 11 December 1942. No 1604 arrived for the ceremony, running light, with the British and American flags crossed in front of the smokebox. Colonel Ryan, the Acting Chief of Transportation of the US Army in Britain, made the formal presentation to Lord Leathers, the Minister of War Transport. In his speech, Lord Leathers referred to '. . . three years of war with steadily mounting traffic have left our fleet of locomotives inadequate to meet the demands upon it' and said he regarded '. . . her as a true and tangible symbol of the co-operation of the United Nations'. Among the many official guests present were the Chief Mechanical Engineers of the LMS, Southern and Great Western, but Edward Thompson seems to have been otherwise engaged, although the LNER chairman, Sir Ronald Matthews, was there. The locomotive concerned was one of the first eight to arrive, and all four main-line companies were to be involved in the commissioning operations as well as operating them. The Southern, with six at Exmouth Junction, had the smallest allocation, although Eastleigh was involved with many for other companies in view of its proximity to the port of Southampton. The Great Western, however, had a large allocation of 175, which actually outnumbered their own 28XX locomotives. Considerable numbers of the American locomotives arrived at the GWR ports in South Wales and, after being commissioned and run in, were stored until required by the US Army.

One of the peculiarly American features on the S160s was the cause of two bad boiler accidents, the first of them occurring on the Great Western near Honeybourne. The US locomotives had only a single boiler water gauge, with try cocks as an alternative, but such an arrangement was of course usual on all Great Western locomotives, which in this respect differed from standard British locomotive practice. However the standard cocks were of the plug variety whose position was immediately visible. The gauges on the American locomotives were fitted with hand-wheels, and the top one was connected to the actual cock by a lengthy rod with a universal joint. As a result, crews did not always realise that the top cock might be partially shut, which caused the accidents, the first of which fatally scalded the fireman. The Honeybourne incident was carefully investigated and special instructions issued to all sheds throughout the country that were operating the S160s, the warning plate below the valve handle being modified to ensure that the valve was '. . . always in the *fully* open position'. Although the driver of the second locomotive to suffer an explosion had been instructed on this particular point, he failed to react to the blowing of the fusible plug in the firebox some three miles before the firebox collapsed, and was thus held responsible for the accident.

The US Army also used 0–6–0Ts for shunting purposes, and some of these locomotives worked briefly on the GWR in the summer of 1944 before they too were shipped to Europe.

Towards the end of the war Swindon itself started building Stanier 2–8–0s, eighty being turned out between June 1943 and July 1945. These were all used on the GWR until late 1946, when it was decided to transfer them to the LMS and replace them with some of the Austerities that had returned from the war.

We have so far confined our discussion of wartime motive power changes to the influx of 'foreign' locomotives on to the GWR, but Swindon were also adding to their home-built

4. After the air raid at Newton Abbot on August 20th 1940. In the foreground a bomb crater has filled with water from a damaged main. The badly damaged Pannier tank, no. 2785, is on the right. It had to be chained to another damaged locomotive beyond it to stop it falling into the crater, but was later cut up on the spot, becoming one of the few GWR locomotives written off during the war.

designs. Although the construction of express passenger locomotives was not allowed during the war, there was no such ban on mixed-traffic ones, and Halls continued to be built steadily throughout the 1940s. Collett retired in 1941 at the age of seventy, and was succeeded by Hawksworth, who made a number of changes to the design so that locomotives from No 6959 onwards were known as the Modified Hall Class. The most obvious change was that the plate frames were continued right through to the front buffer beam, which, although giving a much stronger front end, necessitated the construction of a new cylinder design. Another less obvious change was the introduction of enlarged, three-row, superheaters, starting a significant trend that was subsequently to be extended to other classes. In deference to war-time shortages, the new locomotives were not named, but carried the painted words 'Hall Class' on the centre splashers. The usual brass nameplates were fitted after the war.

As mentioned in part two of this study, the construction of 2–8–0s to Churchward's general designs had been resumed in 1938 after a pause of nearly twenty years, and a further fifty-three were built in the period 1940–42, so Swindon had some additional 2–8–0s of their own design to supplement the various strangers of the same wheel arrangement that came and went during the war years. Ten more 2–8–0 tanks were also constructed in 1940. These were officially re-placements for some of the earlier locomotives of that wheel arrangement which had been altered to 2–8–2Ts in the mid-1930s, but were nevertheless completely new. With the six-coupled designs, 1940 marked the construction of a further twenty of the '2251 class' 0–6–0 tender locomotives, to be followed by another similar batch in the last two years of the war. Far more numerous, however, were the additional pannier tanks that were built during the period,

each year seeing a further batch added to stock. Annual completion rates varied between eighteen in 1941 to thirty-seven in the following year, with a total of 135 over the five years 1940–44.

Although planned and ordered before the war, it was not until 1940 and 1941 that the second-generation of streamlined diesel railcars entered service. Numbered from 19 upwards, they were constructed to more-traditional railway design than their predecessors, with separate bodies and underframes, which had standard drawgear and buffers. The last four cars were single-ended and were designed for operation in pairs at speeds of up to 70 mph. If required, an ordinary coach could be coupled between them, and the necessary control cables were then clipped to its footboards. These units thus set the pattern for the numerous diesel multiple units built after nationalisation. Fifteen of the seventeen new twin-ended cars were limited to a maximum speed of 40 mph, which gave them the capability of hauling a trailing load of up to sixty tons. The remaining two passenger vehicles had a twin-speed arrangement, which provided a 60 mph capability when running solo, with the alternative ability to haul other vehicles when the lower gear-ratio was selected. The batch also included a second parcels car, no 34. All the new railcars had a very different appearance from those built previously, being much more angular in design, the only curved surfaces being the roofs above the cabs. As well as being simpler to construct, the new design also increased the available floor length. An interesting feature with these cars was that there were two pairs of warning horns at each end. One set was operated by the main compressed air system, and the others by independent compressors. They were tuned to E flat and G, the choice of these notes being based on pre-war French practice. Two of the GWR's railcars were lent to the LNER for a period in

5. On December 6th 1940, the 7.10 pm train from Bristol to Salisbury was hit by bombs. Soldiers view the damage next day, perhaps indicating that there were unexploded bombs involved. The locomotive is one of the Churchward Moguls.

1944 and worked local services in the Newcastle area.

The pioneer Great Western diesel-electric shunter was used throughout the war on the oil wharves at Swansea, operating in company with one of the generally similar LMS locomotives which were on loan to the GWR.

Rolling Stock

The construction of new ordinary coaching stock vehicles was kept to a minimum during the war, Swindon turning out only a little over 200 in 1940, and less than half this number in the following year, after which there was a complete stop on new construction until well after the war had ended. The Great Western's stock of passenger coaches remained remarkably constant

23

throughout the war, fluctuating by less than 100, and varying between 5,915 in 1939 and 5,824 at the end of 1944. The number of vehicles overhauled, however, rose dramatically from 11,000 in 1940 to no less than 19,000 four years later, but even so the percentage of vehicles 'under or awaiting repair' rose from 6.87 to 9.20. This was a clear indication of the wear and tear of wartime traffic demands. Shortages of materials doubtless had their effect in delaying the completion, while extra work in the long run would be caused as a result of the need to 'mend and make do' rather than carry out the full repairs necessary.

In addition to such repairs and overhauls there was the frequent need to adapt vehicles for special purposes. The first was to provide casualty evacuation trains intended for use after heavy air raids on large cities, when it was feared that the numbers requiring treatment might swamp the available hospital resources. They were made up of nine bogie vans for the stretcher cases, with three support vehicles. A corridor brake third was provided at each end to accommodate staff and stores, together with the necessary cooking facilities, while a gutted centre-corridor third supplied space for the staff to eat and relax. The conversions were put in hand early in 1939, but the bogie vans were still needed in ordinary service, so the brackets for the stretchers were stored on the underframes of each vehicle concerned. Swindon was one of the seven carriage works involved in the conversions, the Great Western being responsible for six trains. The vehicles to carry the casualties were converted from 'Siphon G' bogie vans usually used for milk churns, but fitted with corridor connections and steam heating. Each could accommodate forty-one stretcher cases, some on the floor, with the rest supported on two lines of brackets fixed to the inside walls. When the final emergency came only three days

were required to locate the vehicles, complete the conversions and move them to their wartime stabling points. A total of thirty-four trains were provided altogether, twenty of them being required for London, with the others sited at strategic points elsewhere. Fortunately they were never used for their intended purpose but found employment with the evacuation of hospitals and other similar institutions. After D–Day some were used to move British and American casualties from the Channel ports to the reception hospitals, and I remember seeing these trains working northwards out of Oxford on the GWR with, if I recall correctly, Southern locomotives in charge.

Early in the war twenty-five ambulance trains were also converted by the railways for military use, twelve of them being for this country and the remainder available for deployment overseas. The Great Western's involvement with these trains was the conversion of eighteen LMS corridor vehicles, twelve for overseas and the remaining six to form administrative cars for the home service trains. Nine of the overseas trains were lost at the time of the Dunkirk evacuation. For the launch of the Second Front in Europe in 1944 thirty-three ambulance trains were provided to travel to Europe for the use of the British and United States forces, some of them being made up of vehicles originally converted for the 1939 casualty-evacuation trains. Hawksworth, 'in the name of the British Railways' handed over the first of these fourteen-car trains in March 1943, one of the S160s being used as motive power for the occasion.

Swindon was also called on to provide the special train used by General Eisenhower as his mobile headquarters before and after D-Day, being moved to the continent after the Allied forces had broken out of the Normandy bridgehead. His train was codenamed 'Alive', while a similar one for General Montgomery, converted at Doncaster, was known as 'Rapier'. Both trains were self-contained, with their own power sources and the full complement of 'Alive' comprised no less than eighteen vehicles. Not all were of GWR origin, the LNER providing a first-class sleeper with four berths removed to form a saloon.

The traditional Great Western liveries suffered from wartime austerity. After 1942 only the Kings and Castles continued to be painted green, but even with these the orange and black lining-out was omitted. All the other classes appeared in plain black. At the same time the traditional chocolate and cream coaching stock livery was abandoned except for the vehicles used for the 'Cornish Riviera' and 'Torbay Express', as well as the streamlined railcars and special saloons. The other vehicles began to appear painted overall in reddish-brown, with a bronze coloured line at the waist. To set against this simplification there was the welcome reappearance of the company's coat of arms on some of the locomotives and coaches, replacing the less-colourful and attractive monogram. Wagon liveries also changed at the same time, general-purpose vans and covered containers being painted in dark brick red, the pigment being a bauxite residue. Open wagons were not re-painted, except for the bottom left-hand quarter board used to record the vehicle's number and other particulars. Insulated and ventilated vans retained their stone colour for distinguishing purposes.

The provision of sufficient freight vehicles was a constant problem throughout the war. By the end of 1943 over 28,000 new ones had been placed in service throughout the network, and the 1944 programme called for the construction of over 13,000 more. In addition, all the 585,000 private-owners' wagons were commandeered by the Government at the beginning of the war. To ensure the maximum use of this fleet it

became impossible to differentiate between wagons from individual owners and in March 1941 a new organisation was set up near Amersham with the imposing title of the Inter-Company Freight Rolling Stock Control. This was responsible for a 'Pool' of no less than 1.2 million wagons, a figure which should be compared with British Railways' stock of 71,000 at the end of 1982. The Great Western's own merchandise and mineral wagon stock increased from 83,000 in 1939 to nearly 90,000 by 1944. Wartime demands resulted in a fall in the number of wagons overhauled each year from nearly 217,000 in 1939 to 187,000 in 1944, while the number of vehicles 'under or awaiting repair' increased from 3.8 to 5.5 per cent over the same period. Although appreciably less of the wagon fleet was unavailable for traffic compared with the passenger coaches, the percentage increase in those stopped for attention was a great deal higher, in spite of the great efforts being made to maintain maximum use.

This is a convenient point in our narrative to discuss the non-railway work carried out in the GWR workshops in support of the war effort. The availability of well-equipped heavy engineering facilities, with a well-trained staff, made all the railway works the obvious places to carry out specialised construction work of various sorts. Swindon, for instance, built anti-aircraft guns amongst many other items. Some were produced in considerable quantities, such as the quick-release equipment for barrage balloons, of which nearly 22,000 were required, while over 100,000 components for anti-aircraft predictors were turned out. Another mass-production job was the manufacture of the first 2,000-pound bombs, the design of which was worked out in conjunction with the Ministry of Aircraft Production. Later the larger 4,000-pound version was developed, and Swindon produced over 2,000 of them, appropriately code-named 'Görings' while the half-size version was known as a 'Göbbels'. It was, of course, only the casing that was produced by the railway workshops, which was no place to handle high explosives, an operation carried out at one of the munition factories 'somewhere in England', which will be referred to later. In the early 1940s Swindon was also comprehensively equipped for the manufacture of wooden-bodied coaches and wagons, and these facilities were also utilised during the war for special jobs, such as the fifty sets of wooden superstructures built to go on what amounted to an oversize torpedo to turn it into a midget submarine. In all, the government work carried out by the Great Western Railway during the war amounted to just over £3.8 million.

Ways and Works

In addition to dealing with routine maintenance and repairing bomb damage, the Great Western's civil engineering staff were called on to carry out or oversee a considerable programme of new works during World War II. During 1939 and 1940 a number of new works were completed which had been started in pre-war days on the railways' own account. These included the new carriage lifting and painting shops at Caerphilly and Old Oak Common, while the reconstruction of Leamington Spa station was completed. Further west, work continued on the rebuilding of Plymouth North Road station, using arc welding for the supports of the platform canopies.

There were, however, many extensive new works undertaken as a direct result of the war, including the moving of the Great Western's headquarters to Beenham Grange near Aldermaston. In the early years most of the new construction was to provide emergency facilities

to prevent heavy air attacks on strategic centres paralysing railway communications over a large area, but latterly they were mainly involved with ensuring adequate rail links to the ports in Southern England as part of the preparations leading up to the Allied invasion of Europe.

Even before the post-war closure of the Snow Hill route between the LPTB widened lines and the Southern at Blackfriars, railway connections across the Thames in the London area were not exactly lavish, and there were great worries about the effect of raids putting one or more of these out of action for extended periods. To meet this danger a new belt line route was constructed, taking a sweep round the capital with a radius of about fifty miles from Charing Cross. It was based on the LMS's Cambridge-Oxford line. New connections were built at Sandy (opened in 1940), Bletchley (1942), Calvert (1940) and at Oxford (1940). Each of these was designed to facilitate through running on or off the belt line for major traffic flows. At Oxford, for example, there had previously been only exchange sidings connecting the LMS line into Rewley Road with the GWR's route northwards to Wolvercote Junction. This was improved by the construction of a completely new double-line junction about half a mile north of the two stations, at Oxford North Junction. As early as 1951 this connection found permanent use when the passenger trains from Bletchley were diverted into the former GWR station, enabling Rewley Road to be closed to passengers, sixteen years before the line itself lost its services in the post-Beeching era.

Trains using the belt line to reach south-east England from the north would cross over to the Southern Railway at Reading. The pre-war connection there consisted of a steeply-graded and sharply-curved line, with a burrowing junction in the southbound direction, and in June 1941 a new flat junction was constructed some-

6. A Dean Goods ready for overseas service with the Army in January 1940. The Westinghouse brake pump and reservoirs can be seen. No 156 was originally GWR no 2529, built in June 1897. A close examination of the original photograph shows a very rough finish with the WD black paint applied over an extensively chipped original livery.

British Rail Western Region

what further to the east. It is this line that is today used by the Manchester–Brighton and other through services, while the electrified tracks that used to lead to the Southern Railway's terminal station are now diverted into the bays (Platforms 4a and 4b) at the London end of the main down platform. Another new connection between the Great Western and Southern was constructed at Staines Moor. This permitted through running off the GWR's branch from West Drayton via Colnbrook on to the Southern's line from Windsor.

The port facilities at Southampton were of great military importance in World War II, and a new connection was provided at the end of the New Docks to give trains off the Great Western, running via Salisbury and Nursling, easy access into the dock area. This was one of the new works constructed in connection with the build-up to the invasion of Europe, and was opened in 1943. Trains from the Midlands to Southampton taking the former LSWR main line via Winchester would have to thread the bottle-neck at Reading. To avoid this, and to provide an alternative route in case the main line should be cut by enemy action, the former Didcot, Newbury & Southampton Junction Railway was upgraded. The whole eighteen miles from Didcot to Newbury were doubled, as well as the first two miles south of that point, beyond which the extra capacity was obtained by lengthening the loops from 300 to 500 yards, with some additional crossing places being provided. A new single-line connection, one mile long, was also built from the former LSWR up line north of Winchester to the DN & SJ, which in effect provided a non-conflicting junction some five miles long, extending from Winchester Junction to Shawford. To carry out all the engineering works necessary, the ordinary passenger train services were suspended for seven months from August 1942, being replaced by railway-associated buses which called only at the stations and halts. The problem of operating points at the far end of the lengthened loops like these without the expense of a new signal box was solved by the installation of electrical point machines, operated by a hand-cranked generator in the existing box. Similar equipment was installed extensively elsewhere on the GWR during the war. On the DN & SJ line the lengthened loops also required the provision of auxiliary single-line token instruments at the end furthest from the signal box.

For the invasion of Europe in 1944 vast quantities of men and materials had to be assembled at ports within easy striking distance of the Normandy beaches, since it was planned to get 130,000 men ashore on the first day of the campaign. Many army convoys arrived by road to be loaded on the landing craft, and inhabitants of Cornish villages were warned that for long periods they might not even be able to cross their own main street because of the endless stream of traffic. Clearly the railway system in the West Country was similarly required to run to capacity and during the war four new connections were constructed between the Southern and GWR. Strictly speaking the first of these, at St Budeaux, was more of an emergency link in case of air raid damage, being opened in March 1941. Within two months the Luftwaffe's night raids had blitzed Devonport Dockyard and the surrounding area, and the existence of the newly-constructed connection was invaluable. Again this connection, originally built for emergencies, has become part of the present-day railway scene since the Gunnislake services now operate over it, and the former Southern Railway route from St Budeaux into Plymouth has been closed. Further new wartime lines built in direct support of the D-Day plans and opened in the autumn of 1943 were those at Yeovil, Lydford and Launceston. The first permitted through running from the GWR's Weymouth line in the direction of Exeter, while the one at Lydford replaced a less convenient connection which had already proved invaluable earlier in the war. At times GWR services between Penzance and Exeter operated via Bodmin Road (now Parkway), Bodmin, Wadebridge, Launceston and Okehampton, which involved no less than four reversals. Another wartime measure of a somewhat different nature in the same area involved the decking-in of the track across the Royal Albert Bridge between St Budeaux and Saltash which would have permitted tanks to cross the Tamar by this route in an emergency.

There were many other instances of railway lines – as distinct from trains – being prepared to play a military role in World War II. After the fall of France, when Britain stood alone, there was great activity to ensure that, if the Germans had invaded, their forces could be contained. Various stop-lines were built, many of them using railway routes, while elsewhere the possibility that the enemy's tanks might use a convenient railway track to outflank a stop-line led to the construction of tank traps across the tracks. Clearly these had to be built so that trains could pass them in normal circumstances, with the gap being closed quickly in the event of invasion. The railways were closely involved with much of this work, especially where the defences were constructed on their own property. Even today it is possible to see the extent of some of these defences. From the former Great Western's main line to the West of England via Castle Cary, the extensive provision of pillboxes can be seen virtually the whole way from the Kennet & Avon Canal to the Grand Western Canal at Taunton. Cogload Junction itself is still dominated by a ring of these concrete structures sited on the summits of the northern cutting slopes. Both ends of the Royal Albert Bridge were also covered by pillboxes.

To return to the new works carried out in World War II, mention must be made of the quadrupling done jointly by the GWR and LMS between Cheltenham and Gloucester. The two companies' separate lines from Birmingham joined at Landsdowne Junction, just west of their respective stations in Cheltenham, and the two-track section continued for six miles to Engine Shed Junction outside Gloucester. This marked the recommencement of multiple tracks with the GWR's Gloucester avoiding line paralleling the LMS's route, now closed, through their station to Tuffley Junction. The two-track bottleneck was also situated on the route between the docks and industries of South Wales and Birmingham via Chepstow and Severn Tunnel Junction, and authority was given for the quadrupling to be carried out in 1941. Robert McAlpine & Sons undertook the civil engineering contract, which included widening the cuttings and embankments, one of each being over 1¼ miles long, as well as extending seven under- and five over-bridges. The new facilities were brought into full operation within the remarkably short time of thirteen months following authorisation being given. For maintenance purposes, the line was divided between the two companies at the mid-point, just west of Churchdown station. As a result, LMS upper-quadrant signalling with colour-light distants

was installed between there and Engine Shed Junction. The GWR, however, used its standard lower-quadrant design at the Cheltenham end, where it was responsible for the new boxes at Landsdown and Hatherley Junctions. These new works complemented the Great Western's own quadrupling also carried out in 1941 between Severn Tunnel Junction and Newport, which was completed in only six and a half months. The contractor was again Robert McAlpine & Sons.

In this section we have only dealt with the new routes that were provided during the war, but vast mileages of additional loops and sidings were constructed throughout the country to facilitate the handling of traffic. To save on materials many of these were constructed with concrete sleeper blocks instead of full-length wooden sleepers, but in contrast to the arrangements a century earlier on railways such as the Stockton & Darlington, tie-bars were provided for every third pair of blocks. One such loop which I remember well was the one across Port Meadow from Wolvercote Junction to Oxford North Junction. For many of the daylight hours much of its two-mile length would be occupied with southbound freights waiting their chance to trundle through the twin-track bottleneck to Didcot. 2–8–0s of various designs with trains of up to 100 wagons would stand there simmering, one behind the other. At times hours would be spent in inactivity before they could move forward slowly as the first train was given the opportunity to run through the centre road at Oxford and on southwards. The occasional locomotive even managed to blow smoke-rings as it picked up the couplings of its train.

To maintain vital communications in the event of bomb damage to the telephone lines, the GWR installed an extensive radio communication system. This consisted of four fixed stations at Castle Bar, Swindon, the evacuated

M. W. Earley Collection, National Railway Museum, York

7. USA 2–8–0 no 2339 at Reading West Junction in 1943.

Headquarters at Aldermaston, and the emergency dock headquarters at Radyr. Nine mobile units were constructed for use on the railway, using withdrawn four-wheel carriages, and these were supplemented by three road units.

As the war progressed, so the demand for travel information increased. The Central Enquiry Office at Paddington, for example, handled a record 166,000 enquiries in July 1944. The telephone section was staffed largely by young girls coming straight from school at sixteen and each recruit underwent a training course lasting three to four months. This predecessor of to-day's Travel Centres was open from 7am to 11pm daily and remained at work even during air raid alerts, when the girls retired under their desks, each complete with her own telephone and tin helmet.

Trains and Traffic

Forty years after the end of hostilities, it is now extremely difficult to imagine exactly how slow trains were in World War II. In our diesel and electric age, we are now so used to travelling at speeds of over 100 mph that even the best performances by steam-hauled trains seem pedestrian. The last years of the 1930s had seen the zenith of the steam locomotive as far as high-speed performance was concerned, the daily mileage of trains in this country scheduled to run at a mile-a-minute or over reaching the 12,000-mark in 1939.

On the Great Western their world record, held by the 'Cheltenham Flyer', had been eclipsed by the down 'Coronation', but the 65-minute booking from Swindon to Paddington still kept them in second place at 71.4 mph start-to-stop. All told they had twenty-four daily expresses running at 60 mph or over between stops in 1939, which was slightly lower than had been the case in the previous year as a result of minor changes such as the inclusion of additional station calls. Speeds of over 85 mph were regularly being achieved in ordinary service.

With the declaration of war in September 1939 all such high-speed running disappeared for the duration. From 1 September that year the railways were busy operating special timetables for the evacuation of children and others from London and the major industrial areas, but later in September each of the companies introduced its wartime timetable. The Great Western operated its evacuation timetables until 25 September, but in the main the new services came into operation a fortnight earlier, passengers being duly warned by the posters issued by the Railway Executive Committee (see illustration 1). Although during the evacuation period '. . . the public had been requested to limit their train travel to essential journeys', this exhortation had disappeared from the later posters, but towards the end of the war would-be travellers were faced with the far more uncompromising slogan 'Is Your Journey Really Necessary?'.

During the first few months of the war numerous changes were made to the railway services and after some of the Pullman services on the Southern had restarted in mid-September, all the companies reintroduced restaurant cars on a limited scale on 16 October. The initial period, known as the 'Phoney War', fortunately provided the railways with a breathing space to settle down to meet wartime conditions, relatively unmolested by air raids. In the light of experience the maximum permitted speed for trains was raised from 60 to 75 mph in December 1939, with the schedules and time-tables being adjusted to take account of this and other changes, as well as the new requirements in support of the forces being deployed at home and overseas. It was not, however, until November 1940 that the rigid speed restrictions during air raid alerts were relaxed from the previous levels of 25 mph during daylight and 15 mph at night. Although the worst of the Blitz was still to come, it was nevertheless obvious that the disruptive effect on railway operations of the presence of enemy aircraft in the vicinity of a route was more than could be allowed to continue, even though there would undoubtedly be an increased risk that moving trains might run into obstructions or bomb craters.

The December 1939 improvements also included the restoration of the Great Western's West of England services via Westbury, all of them previously having reverted to the 'Great Way Round' via Bristol. Even between London and Bristol the best train in the October 1939 timetables had required 2 hours 35 minutes for the 118.3 miles, compared with the pre-War 'Bristolian's' 1 hour 45 minutes. The number of daily services over this route had also dropped by approximately a third. To Penzance the best time increased by 125 minutes to 8 hours 35 minutes, while the total number of trains in both directions decreased from nine to six. These timetable reductions, however, gave a somewhat false picture since regular duplication of some services was taking place on a day-to-day basis. That Great Western peculiarity, the slip carriage, was also withdrawn at the beginning of the war; but, unlike sleeping and restaurant cars, was not to reappear until after the end of the hostilities.

Any description of the conditions facing the railways during the first winter of the war would not be complete without reference to the exceptionally cold weather in early 1940. While the Great Western's operations never extended to northern England, the severity of the weather even in the West of England could be judged by the fact that a tidal stretch of the River Taw at Barnstaple froze sufficiently hard for groups of people to venture out on to it, even on bicycles. The combined effect of the blackout and weather conditions is reflected in the punctuality figures for the period, which are given in Table 1. The figures show the increased number of

trains that operated from February 1940 onward, while the improving weather rapidly returned the punctuality statistics to their more normal wartime levels.

Although the weather in early 1940 had a marked effect on punctuality, the results of the Blitz on London during the following autumn and winter were even more severe. For the four weeks ending 7 December 1940 the average lateness for the West of England services was no less than 105.44 minutes. The published timetables thus give only part of the story of what the travelling public had to cope with during the war, and it is worth quoting the average yearly figures for express trains over these three main routes in Table 2. The Local, Branch and Workmen's trains were much better, their corresponding all-line punctuality never falling below the figure of 7.22 minutes recorded in 1940. It will be apparent from this comparison that the catching of connections in wartime was a chancy business, and travellers venturing on and off the main lines were usually faced with long waits, unless they were lucky enough to catch the train previous to the one intended. There was thus a major problem for passengers, and even the station staff, in identifying the

Table 1 TIMEKEEPING OF WEEKDAY GREAT WESTERN RAILWAY PASSENGER
TRAINS – WINTER 1939/1940
Class A Through Expresses to and from London

	West of England		South Wales		Northern	
Four weeks ended	Number of trains	Average minutes late	Number of trains	Average minutes late	Number of trains	Average minutes late
9 December 1939	704	13.24	408	16.65	576	19.08
6 January 1940	731	36.52	390	38.09	554	37.88
3 February 1940	757	44.52	408	49.68	575	43.65
2 March 1940	884	17.43	456	23.36	744	24.47
30 March 1940★	844	11.70	436	11.59	713	12.45

★ Figures affected by incidence of Easter
Source: GWR General Statistics October 1941

Table 2 TIMEKEEPING OF WEEKDAY GREAT WESTERN RAILWAY PASSENGER
TRAINS – 1938/1945
Class A Through Expresses to and from London

Year	West of England		South Wales		Northern	
	Number of trains	Average minutes late	Number of trains	Average minutes late	Number of trains	Average minutes late
1938	15,722	5.2	6,962	4.71	10,913	4.27
1939★	—	—	—	—	—	—
1940	10,566	45.80	5,110	44.49	8,677	38.58
1941	11,181	38.88	5,083	47.35	8,325	33.42
1942	11,647	17.20	5,227	28.68	8,085	22.91
1943	11,964	14.42	5,542	21.01	8,059	17.02
1944	10,970	22.68	5,105	28.04	8,059	26.07
1945	11,957	14.65	6,422	17.97	8,060	16.71

★ Not available
Source: GWR General Statistics 1941 & 1946

various trains, to overcome which the use of loudspeaker systems on major stations was extended. Women announcers were also introduced at Paddington, experimentally at first, and in reporting this development in 1941, the *Great Western Railway Magazine* recorded that '. . . passengers have commented favourably on the clearness and audibility of their announcements'. Another problem the railway traveller faced was knowing when the required destination had been reached. After 1940, when the possibility of a German invasion of Britain was very real, all destination and identification signs were removed throughout the country to confuse possible enemy paratroops. Station nameboards were included in the ban, but a sign could remain if it was under a roof and could not be seen from the highway or a low-flying aircraft. Out in the open any lettering on station nameboards had to be less than three inches in height, and even then it was only permitted if it could not be seen ' – or understood from a highway, other than the station approach'. It can only be assumed that whoever framed the regulations must have been a commuter on the South-Eastern section of the Southern Railway and aware of the names painted on the roofs of Ashford and Tonbridge stations for the benefit of the London–Paris air services, since it would have required some remarkable feats of low flying to be able to read the average platform-end station sign from the air.

Under war conditions the railways suffered many mishaps and delays that were not of their own causing, and one incident, the aftermath of which I personally observed in the summer of 1944, illustrates what could occur. A Halifax bomber, damaged during a raid over Europe, tried to make an emergency landing at White Waltham, the airfield situated on the south side of the GWR main line between Maidenhead and Twyford. Touching down too late, it overran the grass landing area and crashed into the railway cutting. The wreckage of a four-engined heavy bomber spread across a four-tracked main line would have been bad enough to deal with, but it then caught fire. The airfield fire team was able to rescue the crew, and it was then learnt that the aircraft was still carrying some of its high-explosive bombs, so everyone was ordered

British Rail, Western Region

8. The first of the modified Hall class 4–6–0s, no 6959, after completion at Swindon in March 1944. The straight-through frames can be seen under the smokebox, together with the plate-frame bogie. Unnamed when built, the locomotive later became 'Peatling Hall'.

to the shelters until the heat had caused them to detonate. Extensive damage was done to the tracks by the explosion, as well as to the all-important overhead telephone and signalling lines. Hours after the incident I was able to watch the engineer's trains standing on all four tracks clear of the damaged areas while the permanent way and signalling staff went about their jobs of restoring the line to traffic. Delays, cancellations and diversions must have been widespread on that particular day. Forty years on one wishes that it were possible to give more details of the railway activities involved, but the wartime security measures firmly clamped down on note-taking and photography. More widely publicised was the bad accident at

Norton Fitzwarren in 1940, when the West of England sleeper ploughed through the buffer stops at the end of the relief line due to the driver's misinterpretation of the signals, his concentration being distracted by the damage caused to his home by the Blitz. Twenty-seven people were killed in the resulting pile-up.

It must in no way be inferred that ordinary travel was actively discouraged throughout the whole of the war. *Holiday Haunts* duly appeared in 1940, providing 744 pages for its 6d (2½p) cover-price, and play was again made of the appeal of the 'safe areas, away from sandbags and sirens'. Seat reservation facilities had been withdrawn however, at the beginning of the war, and holidaymakers had to take a chance of finding seats on the train of their choice. It was not until October 1942 that cheap-day tickets were withdrawn generally, but holiday periods still produced their customary peak loadings. In

9. One of the later batch of streamlined railcars under construction at Swindon in October 1939. The photograph, which had been 'Passed by Censor', stated that the railcars were '... being built to supplement the present wartime train services.'

ated by the use of vouchers to enable relatives and friends to visit those evacuated from London. A lot of travel also took place over the wartime Christmas periods, it being quite usual for Paddington to handle an average of 30,000 departing long-distance passengers a day immediately prior to the holiday. This travel peak came slightly later than the postal peak which typically involved some twenty specials each conveying 4,000 bags of mail.

In addition to all this 'optional' or 'leisure' travel as we would describe it today, the railways had to handle increasing numbers of servicemen, in addition to those travelling on essential work. Many thousand special trains were run for the armed forces and their equipment, but these were only arranged when a complete unit required to be moved, and there was a constant flow of small parties or individuals being reposted, going on leave, or even enjoying a 'forty-eight' (a two-day pass). New munitions factories were built that required the conveyance of shift workers by the railways, which also had to handle the raw materials and finished products. One such factory was built near Pembrey in South Wales, in two separate parts, straddling the Great Western main line. During the construction phase, the railway was responsible for moving in 145,000 tons of materials for the second site alone, while during the three-year construction period one nearby rail depot handled half-a-million tons. A peak labour force of 37,000 was planned, and a new four-platform railway station was constructed, complete with two additional signal boxes to handle fifty-eight special trains each day. At the peaks ten departures were timetabled in a twenty-minute period. As many passenger journeys again were made by buses to and from the factory, many of them belonging to railway-associated operators. On the freight side, fourteen wagons of coal were required daily in

1941, although the Government had urged the public not to travel during the August holiday period, the Great Western found itself handling more passengers than in 1939. The number who left Paddington by train on the Saturday before the Bank Holiday was 52,000, the 'Cornish Riviera' running in five portions with a total of 5,000 people. Some of the business was gener-

35

Table 3 GWR PASSENGER TRAFFIC – ORIGINATING JOURNEYS
(excluding season tickets)

Year	Ordinary	Excursion and tourist	Workmen	Other reduced fares	Total
1939	8,342,847	44,765,814	23,503,909	7,906,965	84,519,535
1940	8,413,593	36,506,962	26,386,641	11,863,205	83,170,401
1941	9,487,234	43,308,237	38,962,489	18,133,689	109,891,649
1942	12,261,337	50,287,039	44,202,110	23,329,781	130,080,267
1943	15,770,258	54,417,866	45,811,502	30,352,185	146,351,811
1944	17,211,901	55,026,530	41,383,704	34,056,062	147,678,197
1945	17,134,090	53,129,826	32,697,445	32,794,902	135,756,263

Source: GWR General Statistics 1946

addition to the sixty-four of raw materials, while the finished munitions filled an average of fifty-one wagons every twenty-four hours.

To conclude this résumé of wartime passenger traffic on the GWR I cannot do better than to include Table 3, which gives the numbers of passengers carried during each of the war years. There was a marked drop in excursion and tourist passengers in 1940 compared with the previous year, but thereafter all categories of traffic rose steadily until 1944, with the exception of those buying workmen's tickets, the peak having been reached in the previous year. Between 1939 and 1943 this class of travel nearly doubled, while by 1944 ordinary passengers were up by 106 per cent. Although not quoted in the table, first-class travel virtually quadrupled in this period. First-class facilities were withdrawn from all trains in the London area from October 1941, but since these largely involved season ticket holders, the change would have had little effect on the figures in Table 3. There was an overall increase of about fifty per cent in the average length of each passenger journey during the war, and this factor, coupled with the 23 per cent decrease in passenger train miles on the GWR between pre-war and 1944, goes a long way to explain the crowding that was so often experienced.

There were some withdrawals of passenger services and closures of stations during the war, and the following examples will indicate the sort of changes that took place. The Eston-Portland trains ceased running for some months, but a skeleton service was reinstated in May 1941. Another line was reopened in November 1941 after having been closed for over eleven years. This was the Yealmpton – Plymstock branch, which was reinstated with a service running to the Southern's Friary station to help deal with Plymouth's transport problems after the Blitz. Millbay station was closed in April 1941, and Ford and Lipson Vale halts followed six months later. A number of halts elsewhere on the Great Western were closed at the same time. In the London area the public services to Addison Road, Kensington, ceased in October 1940, while the Brentford–Southall passenger trains were withdrawn in May 1942. Over on the borders of Wales the line from Eardsley to Titley closed in July 1940, and the Hay–Pontrilas branch followed seventeen months later. By and large, however, with petrol severely rationed and not available at all for the private motorist for much of the war, all the railway lines were making a vital contribution to the transport needs of a nation at war. The independent Weston, Cleveland & Portishead Railway closed

10. A train of Sherman tanks in Acton Yard in July 1942. In the distance a Stanier Class 5 blows off steam, probably on a freight for the LMS via Willesden.

in 1940, but although the Great Western had become the principal creditor it was in no way involved in the operation of the railway, although it acquired the locomotive stock. Only two of them were serviceable, and the Great Western thus found itself in the position of operating a pair of the Stroudley Terriers.

While most of us who were around during the 1939–45 period had our own experiences of wartime rail travel, the effect of delays and congestion on the freight side were much less

obvious to the ordinary member of the public, being hidden by the effects of rationing and general shortages. It is consequently far more difficult to present a thumbnail impression of freight operations on the Great Western during World War II. As has already been described, the ordinary wagon stock was operated as a national 'pool', and for that very reason it is difficult to disentangle the Great Western's own share of the proceedings. Reference was made by Charles Hambro, the Chairman, at the 1941 Annual General Meeting, to the frequent complaints about the shortage of household coal, the Great Western having been strongly criticised because

37

it could not load coal available at collieries and ordered by a customer. He had to point out that this particular commodity was not included in the official list of materials for which the railways had to give priority if there was any shortage of wagons or line capacity.

Much was done to alleviate these problems in subsequent years, and we have already discussed the new works carried out to help keep traffic moving. Other steps were also taken to speed the movement of freight, considerable effort being expended to ensure the rapid unloading of wagons so they could be returned to traffic. 'Where there's a will, there's a wagon away' was one of the slogans adopted, while in 1941 there was the 'Q' campaign for the quicker turn-round of wagons. While the railways could only exhort their customers with their own private sidings to speed up these activities, the Great Western put considerable drive into its own operations. Office workers were encouraged to volunteer to unload wagons on overtime or on Saturdays and Sundays. On one particular week-end in the autumn of 1943 a special drive involving the company's own staff, as well as those of traders, resulted in the clearance of 27,394 wagons throughout the system, but in the following January this figure was beaten with a total of no less than 28,659. Earlier on an important change was made to cut down on wagon usage, referred to as 'nominated loading'. After voluntary trials, this was made compulsory in 1941, all those consigning small loads having thereafter to confine their loadings for particular areas to the two or three 'nominated' days each week for which the railway would provide wagons. Not only did this move increase the loads carried by individual vehicles but cut down on intermediate transhipments.

In the main the British people reacted well to the successive turns of the austerity screw, but there was one ban associated with the railways which was eventually withdrawn as a result of public pressure. In November 1942 the Ministry of War Transport forbade the transport of flowers and plants by train. When it was found that they were being sent by post instead, they were banned there too, but, in response to comments in Parliament and elsewhere, individuals were reluctantly allowed to take flowers and plants in the compartment with them as long as 'the railway were in agreement' and they were visible. This led to more questions in the House about the right to search luggage for hidden flowers, and the last straw was when it was discovered that whole lorry-loads of produce were being driven to Covent Garden while trains had space available. In the light of this damning evidence, the Ministry withdrew the ban, and the whole matter was well summed up in the *Railway Gazette*'s editorial which concluded, 'Although we rejoice as members of the public at the slight modification of the austerity campaign, even if it is made towards the end of the spring flower season, we can only hope that any advantages obtained as a result of the original Order have been sufficient to justify the Parliamentary and departmental time occupied on such a comparatively trivial matter. We have our doubts!' As far as the growers in Cornwall were concerned, together with their chief carrier, the GWR, the ban was lifted very late in their season although their competitors in Lincolnshire (and the LNER) were better able to benefit.

Other West Country specialities were, however, well catered for by the GWR. The Cornish Broccoli Growers Emergency Committee was formed in 1940 to coordinate distribution and worked closely with the GWR. With food rationing tightening the nation's belts, the market for rabbits increased considerably in the major conurbations, and the GWR laid on an evening special from Barnstaple to

Table 4 GREAT WESTERN FREIGHT TRAFFIC

Year	Aggregate of all originating freight (millions of tons)	Total loaded wagon miles (millions)	Empty wagon miles (millions)	Loaded wagon miles per empty wagon mile	Total wagon miles (millions)	Total freight train miles (hundreds of thousands)
Pre-war★	53	585	265	2.21	850	247
1940	52	—	—	—	—	269
1941	48	706	218	3.24	924	260
1942	49	725	208	3.49	932	268
1943	51	727	218	3.33	945	271
1944	50	731	221	3.31	952	271
Percentage change 1944 ÷ pre-war	−6	+25	−17	+50	+12	+10

★ September 1938 – August 1939
Source: History of the British Railways during the War 1939–45, R. Bell

Taunton which gave overnight connections to London, Birmingham and the North. As many as 400 hampers were handled in a single night, their combined weight of twenty tons requiring considerable human effort to load and unload. Traditionally the open wicker hampers carried the carcases slung on a series of parallel poles across the top, threaded between the interlaced rear legs of the unskinned animals, up to 15,000 of which reached Taunton at a time.

The results of the Great Western's wartime freight operations are given in Table 4. From the point of view of the tonnages originated, their business fell during the war by six per cent. On the whole of Britain's railways there was an overall six per cent increase, the LMS chalking up an extra sixteen million tons in 1944 compared with the pre-war figure. The location of the country's heavy industry is very much biased to the north and west, and clearly the LMS would be expected to do much of the origination, handing the loaded wagons over en route to other railways. To obtain a better idea of what each railway was actually doing we need to look at the total wagon miles, and with this the Great Western's performance was up by a quarter of what it had been before the war. Even so the three other railways all registered greater percentage increases, with the LMS achieving 1,725 million loaded wagon miles in 1944. From the freight operators' point of view, it has always been vital to reduce empty wagon movements as much as possible, and immediately before the war the Great Western had moved 2.21 loaded wagon miles for every empty one, its next best competitor being the LMS with a figure of 2.18. Under wartime conditions the utilisation of wagons increased very considerably overall, but again the Great Western managed to achieve the best figures in 1944, with 3.31 loaded wagon miles for every empty one, the LMS once more coming second with 2.99. The best GWR performance was achieved in 1942, the figure falling somewhat thereafter, but the company still finished the war with a 50 per cent improvement in this particular performance index. By and large the total freight ton-mileage on the Great Western was fairly constant, varying between 26.0 and 27.1 million miles, compared with a pre-war figure of 24.7.

We have so far discussed general wartime traffic on the Great Western, but there were a number of periods of exceptional activity which cannot be allowed to pass without comment. Mention has already been made of the evacuation of children from the major industrial areas at the beginning of the war. The Great Western was involved in the movements out of six of these, London, Birmingham, Smethwick, Birkenhead, Liverpool and Bootle. The Munich crisis in September 1938 had resulted in hurried plans being drawn up for evacuation specials from the London and the Birmingham areas, but when the crisis had passed relatively few ran, while a naval special carrying 250 ratings from Keyham to Scotland for the mobilisation of the fleet was terminated at Bristol. The experience gained in the autumn of 1938 was immensely valuable in the following year, the Great Western using Ealing Broadway, rather than Paddington as its main London railhead. School children, accompanied by their teachers, arrived on the District and the Central Lines, and fifty main-line train-sets of up to twelve coaches were used to move the parties to the reception areas. The timetable was arranged so that the early departures ran to safe destinations near enough to permit the stock to return for a later working the same day. Fifty-eight trains were worked on the first day, 1 September, and conveyed just over 44,000 passengers, but the planning allowed for a total of sixty-four if required, with departures from Ealing Broadway at nine-minute intervals. After the successful completion of these evacuations in 1938 and 1939, the railways received messages of congratulations from both the Government and representatives of the local authorities, which the Great Western duly passed on to its staff.

In order to maintain family connections,

Photo Source Fox

11. The maintenance of morale amongst workers on the Home Front during the war was an important matter, and, as part of this, George Allison, the well-known Arsenal football manager gave a number of talks to GWR staff during their lunch breaks.

excursions were run later in the winter to enable parents to visit their children. The Great Western started their series of specials in December and 4,000 people were carried on the first Sunday. These services were very popular and the following week the 8.55 am to North Somerset had to run in three parts to accommodate nearly 1,600 passengers.

With the German invasion of the Low Countries in the following May, it was the turn of children from parts of Kent and East Anglia to be evacuated. The Great Western became involved at the receiving end with many movements from the Southern's and LNER's areas, and in mid-June had to cope with the evacuation of close on a further 70,000 children from London. As a result of all this activity during the first year of the war, the GWR ran over 500 specials conveying 285,000 evacuees.

12. The steel cases for 1000-pound bombs being manufactured at Swindon Works during 1941.

British Rail Western Region

Four years later, in June 1944, the first of Hitler's 'secret weapons' fell on London. This was one of the Flying Bombs or V1s, which for the next two and a half months were to subject the capital to another major onslaught from the air. The railways suffered considerable additional damage, but the Great Western was reasonably lucky with only forty-five of the bombs falling near or adjoining their territory, out of a total of over one thousand such incidents in which the railways were involved. The bombing campaign started off three major railway transport operations, the first being the evacua-tion of civilians from London, while for those who had no option but to remain in the front line, nearly 66,000 Anderson and Morrison shelters were transported into London by the railways from all over the country. The railways as a whole moved three-quarters of a million official evacuees from London in 481 special trains, while a further 1,864 additional services conveyed those who left the capital of their own volition. Finally there was the move of the anti-aircraft batteries to the south coast where they could produce barrages of shells to destroy as many of the V1s as possible as they approached the English coast from their launch

13. Broccoli being unloaded at Paddington goods station during April 1942. Women staff are very much in evidence.

sites in the Pas de Calais. This location gave the guns the best possible line of sight, and ensured that the resulting shrapnel fell harmlessly into the sea, leaving the RAF fighters to chase any bombs that got through across the Kent countryside.

It was in the middle of the V1 campaign that an unprecedented event occurred at Paddington. For the first time in its history the station had to be closed to the public. This was on the Saturday before the August Bank holiday, and was because the platforms and Lawn were packed, while the crowds outside were having to be marshalled by mounted police. The Ministry of War Transport had decreed that no extra trains or coaches were to be operated, and in spite of having locomotives and carriages standing by, the GWR could not at first get the Ministry to change its mind. It was reputedly only when Sir James Milne threatened to drive direct to No 10 Downing Street that authority was given for the extra trains to run. Quite apart from the annoyance that the ban would have caused in ordinary circumstances, in 1944 there was the horrific possibility that a flying bomb could at any moment suddenly land in such a vast crowd.

The Great Western was not alone in experiencing such heavy demands for travel on that day, but it was the Government rather than the railway that was the subsequent target of scathing editorials.

These evacuation campaigns were essentially to deal with civilian movements, but the military evacuation from Dunkirk in 1940 was one in which the railways were deeply involved on land as well as at sea. The role of the Great Western's ships at Dunkirk will be described in a later section, dealing with their activities throughout the war as a whole, but back in England the Railway Executive Committee was given the simple instruction to clear the troops from the port areas as speedily as possible after they had been brought back across the Channel. A 'pool' of 186 trains was formed by the four railway companies, the Great Western contributing forty. The Southern Railway was very much in the front line, as the vast majority of those evacuated were landed at their Channel ports, but the trains had to be fanned out from their territory to suitable reception areas throughout the country, where the troops could be moved into accommodation of some sort or other, however temporary, such as the tents hurriedly erected on Port Meadow between Oxford and Wolvercote. All the trains were made up of ten coaches to enable them to be handled by whatever was available in the way of motive power, and it was unfortunate that the Great Western's loading gauge barred their locomotives from working further into Southern territory than Redhill, which nevertheless saw many Moguls and Manors over the nine peak days of the evacuation. Operations were far from straightforward, as suitable stops had to be arranged, not only for the locomotives to take water, but for the troops to be fed. During this period 565 military specials were run to handle almost 300,000 troops. Once again

one wishes that detailed notes could have been made of the movements involved.

After the rearguards maintaining the beach-head at Dunkirk had finally surrendered, the German armies turned southwards into France, and a further evacuation of British and Allied troops took place from the ports along the Brittany coast. This time it was the Great Western's turn to receive those returning, and more than two hundred specials were run from Plymouth and other ports in the South-West. The railways' role in these vital military operations was widely appreciated and many tributes were paid to the unstinted efforts put in by the staff of all grades and departments at this critical stage of the war.

Four years later, when the Allied forces returned to the Continent on D-Day, the railways again played a vital role in their movement and that of their equipment. These could, of course, be planned much more in advance, but it should not be overlooked that the V1 offensive began just one week after the first of our troops had landed in France, diverting the railways' attention and resources away from the task of keeping munitions and reinforcements moving to the Channel ports, while another 600 specials were taking bombs to the airfields to maintain the air attack on Germany and their military installations. In the three weeks immediately preceding D-Day no less than 9,679 specials were run, although this figure probably includes the element of multiple-counting by each separate railway company which complicates all wartime statistics on this particular subject. The build-up had started at the end of March, and during this longer two-month period the total number of specials topped 24,000, and conveyed 230,000 men, this time complete with 12,000 tons of baggage, in marked contrast to the situation at the time of Dunkirk. Three million gallons of petrol a day in bulk and cans had also to be conveyed to the ports to keep the armies' mechanised equipment mobile. Luckily the changed fortunes of war no longer made it necessary to ensure that all bulk stocks of fuel were withdrawn more than thirty miles from the coast overnight, as had been the case in 1940–41. Another new traffic for the GWR developed in the month following D-Day as the numbers of captured German forces reaching England required the provision of over 160 special trains to take them to their prisoner of war camps. All told, in the four weeks following 6 June 1944, 17,500 specials were run for military purposes, not to mention the 113 required for the forces' mail, while some 300 additional journeys were made by ambulance trains conveying the wounded from the ports to hospitals. The Great Western could justly be proud of their share in support of operation 'Overlord' but the wear and tear on their equipment and system were to have their effect on the rate of recovery a year later after peace had been declared in Europe.

Docks and Maritime Activities

During World War II the Great Western's docks and marine activities greatly aided the war effort, but in both cases their main contributions were very different from their peace-time uses. This was in contrast to the main railway operations which essentially constituted an intensification of the GWR's normal activities.

The Great Western's docks on the north side of the Bristol Channel had been built mostly for the export of coal, but, as we saw in earlier volumes, they had developed other roles, including the import of foodstuffs. The German air raids on these ports were undoubtedly in support of their overall campaign to starve Britain out, but the GWR docks continued to perform this vital function throughout the period of hostilities, as well as dealing with new types of cargoes, like tanks and locomotives, which required special handling. There was also a considerable increase in the quantities of general cargo exported, although the coal shipments were to plunge catastrophically during the war. Table 5 gives the overall figures, year by year, for the six principal railway ports.

Table 5 IMPORTS AND EXPORTS AT THE GREAT WESTERN'S
SOUTH WALES PORTS
(Newport, Cardiff, Penarth, Barry, Port Talbot and Swansea)

| Year | Imports | Exports | | Total | Overall Total |
	tons	Coal and coke tons	Other traffic tons	tons	tons
1939	4,836,801	18,858,108	1,881,959	20,740,067	25,567,868
1940	5,121,587	13,098,834	1,765,310	14,864,144	19,985,731
1941	4,081,596	8,240,734	1,876,493	9,917,227	13,998,823
1942	3,974,649	8,250,475	2,102,046	10,352,526	14,327,170
1943	5,266,137	7,627,352	2,308,994	9,936,346	15,202,483
1944	5,892,183	5,541,607	3,996,196	9,537,803	15,229,986
1945	3,739,477	4,916,405	3,441,171	8,357,576	12,097,053

Source: GWR General Statistics, 1946

14. Maidenhead station in July 1941, showing the small name-boards used during the war. In addition to the ones on the windows and above the waiting-room door, there is another, yet smaller, version under the heavily-shaded lamp by the Stephen's Ink advertisement.

15. The 'girl announcer' at Paddington station in February 1941. In her hand is a sheet giving the altered platform arrangements for that day. The 10.30 am as well as the 1.55, 3.20, 4.15 and 5.15 pm were all being run in two portions.

Within two years of the start of the war the quantities of coal being put on board ships had plunged to half the pre-war total. Broadly-speaking the reduction was proportionately the same at most of the ports, although Penarth, where the enclosed dock had been shut in 1936, maintained its throughput and even showed a slight increase in 1940. On the other hand, Port Talbot's share of the business fell more than most, dropping from approximately 1.5 million tons in 1939 to less than a third of this two years later, and although there was then a rise for the next two years, by 1944 the port was handling only just over a fifth of the amount of coal it had dealt with in 1939. The big reduction in the demands for the shipment of coal came in the true export market, which fell from 16.5 million tons in 1939 to 1.1 million in 1944. The fall was very rapid indeed, with the loss of over 12 million tons in the first two years of the war. Clearly, however, the U-boats and magnetic mines acted as a powerful deterrent to foreign vessels wanting to come and obtain coal from South Wales. Coastwise shipments, on the other hand, only fluctuated over the smaller range of 2.4 to 4.6 million tons per year. These particular movements would have eased the demands made on the railways for the movement of coal for the war effort. Except in so far as the production at the Welsh collieries fell during the war, the railways were called on to move to inland destinations throughout Britain those tonnages which before they had merely trundled down to the nearest docks and loaded on the next convenient ship. In 1941, for instance, the new passenger timetable that applied from 5 May was out of date before it appeared, as a week earlier a number of main-line trains in South Wales, including one Paddington-Swansea working and its return, were cancelled to enable more coal and freight trains to be handled. Earlier than this however, there had

been a crisis in the South Wales docks which were proving unable to handle the Lease-Lend supplies arriving from the United States, and C M Jenkin Jones from the LNER was moved in to sort the problem out.

The Bristol Channel docks later played a big part in the arrival of war equipment from the United States. As has already been mentioned, many of the USA 2–8–0 freight locomotives were landed in South Wales. Handling heavy loads such as these and army tanks provided problems for the ports, but at times the vessels arriving were equipped with their own high-capacity lifting gear. The SS 'Lakehurst', for instance, could deal with loads of up to 120 tons using its own equipment, and on one occasion turned up at Newport with no less than thirty-four locomotives on board, having appeared with a load of 166 tanks on her previous voyage. There was, however, a need for additional lifting gear at the South Wales ports generally, and various additions to the facilities were made during hostilities.

The Great Western's shipping services, like the Southern's, were badly disrupted during the war and every one of its ships was directly involved in one way or another. The Channel Islands services ceased completely from 28 June 1940 until 18 September 1945 because of the German occupation, but passenger services from Weymouth had ceased at the outbreak of war. The 'St Julien' had been requisitioned immediately as a troop carrier, but was later converted to a hospital ship, as were the 'St David' and 'St Andrew' from the Irish routes. The 'St Helier' had moved across to Fishguard early in the war, but was then taken over for Government service, operating out of Southampton and carrying troops, mail and cargo to Cherbourg and Le Havre. Like the hospital ships, in this role she retained her civilian crew and officers.

When it became necessary to evacuate the British Expeditionary Force from Dunkirk, all four of the Great Western's ships already mentioned were involved in the operation, together with their Channel Island cargo vessels 'Roebuck' and 'Sambur'. The 'St Helier' made no less than seven trips to Dunkirk, after an earlier one to Calais, and brought back nearly 12,000 people to England. She shot down one German aircraft in mid-Channel and was involved in two separate collisions whilst manoeuvring amongst the other ships engaged in the operation. The first of these involved a minesweeper which crossed her bows, and in order to cut down the inflow of water into the latter's hull, the 'St Helier' went ahead slowly at half speed for over half an hour until a tug arrived to assist the damaged minesweeper. One of the paintings by Charles Pears depicting railway steamers in operation during World War II shows the 'St Helier' at night, silhouetted against the fires of the burning port, the damage to her bows being plainly visible. One of the Associated Press cameramen also caught a most dramatic picture of the 'St David' alongside one of the quays, her white hull and superstructure contrasting with the black smoke from the burning oil installations. The smallest vessel in the Great Western's fleet only just failed to get to Dunkirk to play her part in helping with the evacuation. This was the 'Mew', built in 1908, which normally shuttled across the Dart from Dartmouth to Kingswear, and when the call came duly set off up Channel from her base in South Devon at her maximum speed of ten knots. By the time she had arrived in Dover, however, the evacuation was virtually complete and the naval authorities decided she should remain in home waters. The 'Roebuck', joined by the 'Sambur', then moved down Channel to take part in the evacuation from Brittany. Attempting to enter St Valéry to establish contact with anyone on shore, they were both heavily engaged by enemy guns and suffered considerable damage, a number of their crews being killed or wounded.

In the Irish Sea the 'St Patrick', after a short period as a troop transport, continued to operate the service between Fishguard and Rosslare thrice weekly in each direction. In 1940 she was twice attacked from the air without serious damage, although one member of the crew died on the first occasion. On the morning of 13 June 1941, however, she was bombed and sunk with the loss of thirty lives, including the captain and seventeen members of her crew. Several of the passengers owed their survival to the efforts of Miss Mary Owen, one of the stewardesses aboard, whose efforts were subsequently marked by the award of the George Medal. She also received the Lloyd's War Medal, as did the Second Engineer and the Wireless Operator, the latter being awarded the MBE as well. The 'Great Western' continued on the Waterford service until April 1944, but because of wartime conditions this could only be operated twice-weekly after the summer of 1940. She twice fought off attacks by enemy aircraft and from May to August 1944 was used as a troopship in support of the Allied invasion of Europe. Other vessels took over the Rosslare route until June 1942 when the service was suspended after the passenger facilities had been withdrawn six months earlier. As a result, the passengers on the Great Western's Irish services dropped from 136,000 in 1939 to a mere 557 in 1942, although there was thereafter a slight recovery in numbers, solely as a result of the passengers that were handled over the Christmas periods in 1943 and 1944. Normality began to return in the summer of 1945, but even during the war years considerable quantities of other traffic continued to be carried, with, for example, 60,000 head of livestock coming across from Ireland in 1942.

16. With the blackout and other air raid precautions, Paddington was a somewhat gloomy station in World War II. Crowds line the platforms on July 12th 1944 during the flying-bomb attacks on London.

The three Great Western hospital ships moved to the Mediterranean in the summer of 1943, being used in support of the Sicilian and Italian campaigns. The speed and manoeuvrability of the railway vessels made them an excellent choice for such operations, although they were at times involved in voyages of 1,000 miles in marked contrast to their usual cross-Channel trips. On 24 January 1944 the 'St David' was bombed and sunk off the Anzio beachhead, some of those aboard being rescued by the 'St Andrew'. In the summer of the same year the latter was damaged by a mine but managed to reach Taranto and later returned to Britain for repair.

In preparation for D-Day, three of the Great Western's steamers were taken over by the

Forces for use off the beaches of Normandy. These were the 'St Helier', 'Roebuck' and 'Sambur', the latter pair being used to assist the Royal Engineers in manoeuvring the concrete caissons used to form the temporary harbour off Arromanches. The 'St Julien' was one of the hospital ships active in the English Channel after D-Day, but was twice badly damaged, once by a mine and later in a collision.

The ocean liner business at Plymouth ceased early in the war, and three of the tenders used to meet the ships in the Sound were duly taken over by the Admiralty for service in 1939, leaving only the 'Sir John Hawkins' still based at Millbay Docks where she was badly damaged during one of the air raids on Plymouth. After repair she too was taken over for naval service.

A world away from these heroic deeds at sea, the third branch of the Great Western's waterborne activities – the canals – prospered no better or no worse than it had done in peacetime. Wartime initially saw a slight reduction in the tonnages carried on the Kennet & Avon Canal, but the trade had recovered by 1943, although the quantities passing over the Stourbridge Extension dropped slightly. These were the only two of the nine enterprises for which the annual carrying statistics were even worth quoting in the GWR's own booklet, and the Great Western actually made up its mind to abandon the Stover Canal in 1943 as a consequence of the lessees terminating their agreement. At a Special Annual Meeting it was agreed to apply to the Minister of War Transport for a warrant under an act of 1888 which would authorise the abandonment of the canal and release the company from the liability of maintaining it. This canal was only about two miles long, running from Teigngrace station on the Newton Abbot-Moretonhampstead line, to a tidal tributary of the Teign, but the Great Western appears to have been unsuccessful in its bid since the receipts and expenditure statistics continued to appear, and it appears in the list of canals owned in the final (1947) GWR report. Overall the annual loss on the Great Western's canals remained just over £30,000 throughout the war, which represented over twice the total receipts.

Road Activities

With petrol supplies at a premium in Britain during World War II, there was a very slight fall of fifty-six in the numbers of the Great Western's road vehicles between 1939 and 1945, in marked contrast to the rapid expansion that had taken place during the previous two decades. This was not typical of the railways as a whole, the road vehicle stock of the other companies increasing slowly throughout the war. On the other hand, only the LMS increased the number of its 'Horse-Drawn Parcels and Goods Road Vehicles', the Great Western's stock decreasing from 2,827 in 1939 to 2,437 in 1944, while the 1,584 horses used to haul road vehicles in 1939 had dropped to just over 1,100 six years later. While the above figures convey an impression of the availability of the Great Western's motive power on the roads, their stock of 'Parcels and Goods Miscellaneous Vehicles' rose by over 400. Many of these undoubtedly constituted the specialist equipment used to move exceptional loads by road to their final destinations from the nearest railhead.

A review of the company's road transport achievements was published in late 1943, with the figures being shown as percentages of those achieved in 1938. A very marked increase in the productivity of the road motor fleet was obtained during this period. The number of 'cars' at work was virtually constant between 1939 and 1943, but the tonnages handled increased by nearly 20 per cent. The latter year's performance was to represent the peak, however, and carrying fell off later in the war, but every year still saw well over five million tons being conveyed by the 'Company's Motors', while their horse-drawn cartage handled a million tons in addition. The costs of the operation, however, rose significantly during the war, the 1939 motor cartage figure of 3s 9d (18.75p) per ton rising to 4s 7d (23p) by 1944, and to 5s (25p) a year later. Overall horse cartage was appreciably more expensive throughout, but that does not necessarily imply that savings could have been made had the necessary investment in additional motor vehicles been made. Horses undoubtedly were used for the shorter-distance workings with smaller consignments. A reorganisation in November 1942 brought the Great Western's cartage services directly under the control of the Goods and Traffic Departments.

Many unusual loads were handled by the Great Western's road fleet during the war. For instance pipes were off-loaded for 150 miles across the country in the right position beside the trench that had been dug to take them, while 50,000 tons of cement would be required for an airfield, to be delivered to the site at a rate of 400 tons per day. It was even considered to be part of the railway's operations in those days to quote for the installation of a 30-ton boiler on its base inside a power house. Not all the loads handled, however, were big and heavy. In the summer of 1940 Malvern College was moved from Blenheim Palace back to its normal home: no less than 140 tons of effects were involved, and at the delivery end of the journey delivery of each item was required at the correct one of the twenty-five separate destinations in Malvern. Masters and pupils of the school helped with the loading of the road vehicles at Blenheim, and no less than seventy-six wagons and six containers were used. Containers were also used extensively for the earlier removal of works of art from the National Gallery and elsewhere in London to their secret and safe wartime storage sites, police guards being provided, as was the case thirty-five years later when the bulk of the small exhibits from the Museum of British Transport at Clapham were moved to York prior to the opening of the National Railway Museum. The November issue of the *Great Western Railway Magazine* quoted a letter from Mr Kenneth Clark, as he then was, in which he conveyed to the GWR the appreciation of the Trustees of the National Gallery after they had held their first wartime meeting and had been told of '. . . the special facilities you had given us, the amazing regularity with which all our loads went off and the great care with which they were handled. . .'.

Hotels, Restaurant Cars and Refreshment Rooms

The war brought mixed fortunes to the Great Western's catering and hotel activities. As already described, all restaurant cars were withdrawn at the beginning of the war. Although there was a partial restoration in the months that followed, from December 1941 five pairs of trains on the Great Western lost their restaurant car facilities once more, and the railway announced that all such services were being withdrawn during Christmas week to ensure the maximum seating capacity. The following May there was a further cut-back in the level of ordinary services, and finally they were all once more completely suspended in April 1944 during the run-up to D-Day.

The wartime traveller had to eat, however, and there was in consequence a great increase in the refreshment facilities provided on stations, which were used very extensively. On the Great Western the refreshment room receipts in-

Photo Source Fox

17. The day Paddington closed. On July 29th 1944 the crowds wanting to get away from the flying bombs in London for the August Bank Holiday weekend were so great that the station had to be closed. Sir James Milne's direct intervention with the Ministry of War Transport was necessary to enable the GWR to use the extra locomotives and rolling stock that were available.

18. The 'St Julian' as a hospital ship in Cardiff Docks during July 1944. In the background barrage balloons fly above the city.

British Rail Western Region

Table 6 VISITORS AT GREAT WESTERN HOTELS

	Paddington		St Ives		Fishguard	
Year	Number of visitors	Percentage of 1939 figures	Number of visitors	Percentage of 1939 figures	Number of visitors	Percentage of 1939 figures
1939	44,269	100	24,598	100	3,652	100
1944	158,337	358	30,906	126	8,600	235

Source: GWR General Statistics 1946
It is assumed that the figures quoted for 'number of visitors' equate to what these days are referred to in the travel industry as 'bed-nights'

creased from just over £460,000 in 1939 to £1.1 million by 1944.

Somewhat surprisingly the number of visitors at the company's three principal hotels increased throughout the war. While the slower train services would have been expected to lead to more people staying overnight on business trips to London, the same factors would not have been at work at St Ives and Fishguard. The increase was quite marked at all three, however, as the figures in Table 6 show. While the percentage increase was greatest with the Royal Station Hotel at Paddington, the extra visitors at the other two hotels were quite substantial. For the Tregenna Castle the year 1943 had actually been substantially better than 1944, being 62 per cent up on the pre-war figures, which remained remarkably constant throughout the 1930s. An interesting feature of the Tregenna Castle's performance was the relatively small seasonal swings throughout the war, which is again an unusual feature for a hotel at a holiday resort. Its excellent facilities and outlook would undoubtedly have appealed to anyone visiting Western Cornwall on business, particularly since for short visits hotels would not require the production of any ration coupons. The maximum price that could however be charged for any restaurant or hotel meal was fixed at 5s (25p). The Manor House Hotel at Moretonhampstead was requisitioned in the autumn of 1940 and not reopened to visitors until 1 October 1946, while the armed services used part of the Fishguard Bay Hotel.

Mention must also be made under this heading of the additional feeding facilities provided for the railway staff as part of the national policy that also saw the introduction of municipally-run British Restaurants. Early in the war the Great Western introduced mobile canteens for use in connection with emergencies resulting from air raids. Road and rail versions were produced. The former was based on a six-ton articulated Scammell lorry and was virtually self-contained, with supplies of dried foods stored on it and a 125-gallon water tank, so that it could be put straight into service whenever it was required. A clerestory passenger vehicle, No 1823, formed the rail-mounted 'Emergency Canteen', which was provided with gas lighting, with oil-lamps as back-up. Presumably its refrigerated cupboard was also powered by gas.

The importance of wartime communal feeding arrangements was emphasised by the fact that there was even a Main Line Railway Canteens Association, and the Secretary of that

19. Wartime activity at Cardiff Docks. In November 1944 WD 'Austerity' 2–8–0s are being loaded by a floating crane for transport to Europe where they were used on the rehabilitated tracks behind the Allied bridgehead.

organisation was present at the Great Western's West London carriage sidings on 1 June 1943 when a 'mobile trailer kitchen unit' was handed over on behalf of the citizens of Guelph and Wellington County in Ontario, Canada. This was the first such unit to be allocated to the GWR and the ceremony was marked by the presence of a contingent of the GWR Home Guard, while 'King George VI' posed in the background, appropriately ornamented with the British and Canadian flags. In the following April two more mobile kitchens were presented to the GWR Chairman at Paddington, the gift, this time, of the non-British railwaymen of the Buenos Aires Western, the Buenos Aires Great Southern and the Buenos Aires Midland Railways of Argentina.

In May 1944 a new residential hostel and canteen for the GWR's staff was opened at Didcot. It was '. . . by far the largest in the long chain of establishments erected on the Company's system for the wartime welfare of the staff; its chief feature – the inclusion of full residential facilities – makes it the first of its kind'. It was open twenty-four hours a day, and its hundred sleeping cubicles and dining facilities were in part a replacement of the static sleeping and restaurant cars that had been used hitherto. Many railwaymen had been moved to Didcot as a result of its increased importance as a traffic centre, and there was not sufficient permanent housing in the area to accommodate them. The significance of the new facilities was underlined by the involvement of Sir Alan Anderson, the Controller of the Railways and Chairman of the Railway Executive Committee, in the opening ceremony. Another canteen for GWR staff had been opened a month earlier, at Slough. Although without residential facilities, it could seat 108 at any time and the 'commencing membership' was some 850, indicating the scale of GWR employment in that town.

Air Services

The Great Western Railway's involvement in air services has been described in Part Two of this book. As a result of their activities in the 1930s, the railway companies generally built up considerable holdings in the air transport business. After the fall of France, the Railway Air Services' operations during the war were confined to the routes to Belfast from Liverpool and Glasgow. These were, however, outside the sphere of influence of the Great Western, but that company was nevertheless involved with the service operated by another subsidiary, the Great Western & Southern Air Lines, to the Scilly Isles from Land's End. The airfield used was actually only just outside St Just, and the route was to continue in operation under BEA auspices until the introduction of the present helicopter operation from Long Rock.

Vast technical improvements took place with aviation during World War II, and the significance of this was not lost on the railway companies which increased their holdings in the various British airlines during this period under the new Associated Airways Joint Committee. The railways' contribution to the British domestic airline network was stressed in the 1944 official railway publication 'British Railways in Peace and War', and their post-war expansion was one of the plans featured in the final chapter, entitled 'Post War Service'. Under a photograph showing a de Havilland Albatross flying over the streamlined 'Duchess of Hamilton' disguised as 'Coronation', reference was made to the railways' ten years of experience in the field, and their plans for '. . . a wide expansion immediately conditions are suitable, and up-to-date airliners with a high standard of safety and comfort are available to handle the traffic which it is confidently anticipated will desire this method of transport in the post-war era'. Refer-

British Rail Western Region

20. GWR road vehicles at Paddington in September 1943. The Scammell Mechanical Horse on the left has had its solitary headlight removed, while one of those on the right-hand Bedford carries the wartime blackout mask. The real horses on their 4-ton dray seem to be impatient to be on their way.

ence was made to the fact that 'over-water services show the greatest saving of time and convenience'. They also provided least competition with the railways themselves! As a practical step towards this end, Commander G. O. Waters, the General Manager of the Jersey & Guernsey Airways, was granted leave from the Admiralty in the autumn of 1944 '. . . to carry out the preliminary organisation for the restoration of Civil Air Services to the Channel Islands as soon as circumstances permit'. That particular airline had been jointly owned by the Great Western and Southern Railways, which were thus actively taking steps towards the new

Photo Source Fox

21. During the war GWR had three mobile fire-fighting trains. Each had accommodation for a crew of eight, and a pair of trailer pumps which could easily be lowered to ground level and manhandled to the scene of the fire. Most of the trailer pumps during the war were not as mobile as this, and were manned by local teams of volunteers.

developments of peacetime well before the end of the war in Europe.

By the time George Dow came to write the companion volume 'It Can Now Be Revealed' in 1945, the Government had already published a White Paper proposing the formation of a new European Air Company. This was to include the involvement of the British Overseas Airways Corporation, the railways, the short sea shipping lines, the independent air operators, and travel agencies, and thus recognised the British railways' contributions to civil aviation in this country together with their operating experience. However, as we shall see later, the political doctrines of the new post-war Government were to result in widespread organisational changes in all forms of transport, railways and airlines included.

Staff

Between 1939 and 1945 the total number of staff employed by the Great Western Railway increased from 99,223 to 112,102, a rise of 13 per cent. This figure is far less than the increase in traffic carried, which is not surprising in view of the great demands made on the country's human resources during the war years. As with other industries, the railways only kept going by taking on large numbers of women who carried out many jobs that in pre-war days had been a male preserve. The *Railway Magazine* in 1943 published a photograph showing 'representatives of the 16,000 women now employed in numerous grades on the Great Western Railway'. Standing on the footframing of a 4–6–0 or on the platform alongside are twenty-two women, most of them in uniforms of one type or another, each of them carrying a notice indicating her job on the railway. Station staff were represented by a porter, trolley driver and ticket-collector, while a guard and dining-car attendant showed that certain of the train crew duties, in the widest sense, were also covered.

Many of the women came from the railway workshops where they were involved in numerous different trades, but these must, at best, have been employed as relaxees rather than fully-trained tradesmen (no one would have referred to tradespersons in those days). No women had worked in Swindon in pre-war days, but a carefully organised programme of introduction was carried out early in the war, starting with the limited amount of repetition work that was available to ease the training problems required. Ultimately they were to be employed as crane drivers, initially of the walking variety but were later moved to the overhead kind. Welding work was undertaken, too, and some worked as hammer boys in the forge. It must be admitted, however, that the Southern Railway managed to upstage the Great Western when it came to publicising the female staff employed in locomotive works. Their widely-travelled photograph of one of the USA 2–8–0s being commissioned at Eastleigh had a young woman in her overalls leaning out of the smokebox and tightening one of the nuts on the Westinghouse pump.

For the staff of any large organisation during the war there were other duties of national importance which involved them in their own time. The Home Guard was typical and thousands joined the Great Western's own units. In the summer of 1941 some of them were being inspected by the Chairman, Sir Charles Hambro, and in typical Great Western style silver challenge cups were presented as trophies to stimulate proficiency in various different drills. K. W. C. Grand, the Principal Assistant to the General Manager, was closely involved with the force, becoming a Colonel and the company's liaison officer. Four of the sixteen pages of the December 1944 issue of the *Great Western Railway Magazine* were devoted to the final parades of some of the railway's Home Guard units, together with numerous messages of thanks from senior railway officers, politicians and army commanders. General Sir Frederick Pile's words were a reminder that some of the Home Guard had helped to man anti-aircraft gun batteries and thus took an active part in the country's defences whenever raids occurred in their areas.

Another spare-time activity that involved many railwaymen during the war was fire-watching, which subsequently led to the formation of trailer-pump units able to fight quite extensive fires if the National Fire Service had its resources fully committed after a raid. Again, the Great Western stepped in and presented trophies for the men's and women's teams in the All-Line Trailer Pump Competition which was organised on an annual basis. The company had

22. The Castle class 4—6—0 no 5071, renamed 'Spitfire' in September 1940, to mark the GWR's successful National Savings Campaign. When built in June 1938, this particular locomotive carried the nameplates 'Clifford Castle' which were reused in 1946 for the first of the Castles to be constructed after the war. The plated-in side window of the cab will be noted.

long realised that friendly rivalry of this sort not only increased efficiency but boosted morale, and those long-standing stalwarts, the All-Line Passenger and Goods Train Competitions, referred to in earlier volumes, could not be held in wartime conditions.

National Savings were another field where friendly rivalry was used as a stimulus to the campaign. Early in the war numerous communities and organisations had subscribed (rather than lent) to their local Spitfire fund, a figure of £5,000 having been fixed as the nominal cost of 'purchasing' one of these aircraft. The Great Western Railway launched their own campaign to buy one in late 1940, the directors between them personally subscribing the first £500. Contributions were received from every part of the system and the total was raised by the summer of the following year. In the same patriotic spirit, the names of twelve of the Castle class 4–6–0s were changed to those of RAF aircraft, the first, No 5071, naturally being 'Spitfire'. The continuing savings drive was stimulated at intervals by special campaigns, such as 'Salute the Soldier' or 'Warship Week', and the various savings organisations were encouraged to set their members targets to attain, whether in stamps, certificates or defence bonds. The totals achieved even today seem quite spectacular, such as the Swindon target of £15,000 in one campaign in 1944, which was beaten with a total of over £23,000.

Reference must also be made to the 'Dig for Victory' campaign when we were all exhorted to grow more fruit and vegetables to help make up for the rationing and replace the produce from overseas which was prevented from reaching the country as a result of the U–boat activities. Railwaymen were particularly well placed in this respect because of the traditional railway allotment, a patch of ground on the lineside or elsewhere which was rented to an employee for a nominal sum. Even some of the grounds of the new Didcot hostel were set aside for 'horticultural purposes'. Again the company actively encouraged the national campaign, and the *Great Western Railway Magazine* for October 1944 reported the results of no less than seven horticultural shows organised by GWR staff in different centres. In many cases the produce on display was subsequently auctioned for the company's 'Helping Hand' or Comforts Fund.

Finally, in this review of wartime staff activities on the Great Western, mention must be made of those who served in the armed forces. The number early in 1945 reached 15,432, inclusive of those on full-time Civil Defence duties. The total number of employees who served in the forces during the war was, of course, greater than this, and, in addition to the large numbers wounded, nearly a thousand were killed in action or on active service, bringing the total for two World Wars to 3,312.

2

The Final Years

When fighting in Europe ceased on 8 May 1945, the remaining hostilities against Japan were half a world away. After nearly six years of war Britain was anxious to get back to normality as quickly as possible, a wish which was reinforced by the quicker-than-expected Japanese surrender after the dropping of the atomic bombs on Hiroshima and Nagasaki. The railways were not left out in this desire to do new and better things, but the immediate post-war years were to see continuing austerity, with bread rationing being introduced, a measure which had not even occurred during the worst years of the U-boat campaigns. In the summer of 1946 the *Great Western Railway Magazine* was passing on Sir Stafford Cripps' appeal for 100,000 more tons of waste paper, and the GWR responded with its own new salvage drives, as it had done during the war years, when a special exhibition coach had toured the system.

Fuel had become a major problem during the latter years of the war, with those being called up for National Service being offered the opportunity of coal mining as an alternative to joining the armed forces. The coal supply situation was made worse by the terrible winter of 1947, when domestic and office electricity supplies were cut every morning and afternoon. One GWR pannier tank at Colbren Junction stuck in a drift and was completely buried by snow, which finished up a foot or so above the chimney, dome and cab. The *Railway Magazine* for March/April that year had a footnote warning readers of a possible delay in delivery as a printing ban had been imposed and it was not known when the finishing stages would be permitted. When, at the end of the long freeze-up, the thaw finally came, floods took over as the natural hazard facing the railways. East Anglia suffered worst, but the Great Western line was completely submerged at Hinksey, just south of Oxford. On the railway itself coal had deteriorated in quality and risen in price. The overall average consumption rose from 44.21 pounds per mile in 1939 to 55.18 in 1944, wartime congestion also contributing, as shown by the fall to 53.86 pounds per mile in 1945. However, the rising price more than covered this, so the cost per engine-mile rose from 10.78d to 11.88d (4.49p-4.95p) between 1944 and 1945, compared with 4.44d (1.85p) in 1939. Even with the Great Western's concern for the prospects of South Wales generally, which we will discuss at a later stage, it was not perhaps surprising that they were to experiment extensively with oil firing of locomotives in the post-war period. In the prevailing economic conditions there was no way they could involve the electrification bogey this time round. Even the LNER's two pre-war schemes were held up still further, the Shenfield

Millbrook House Collection/P. M. Alexander

23. No 1020 'County of Monmouth', one of the high-pressure, 2-cylinder 4–6–0s constructed by the GWR after the war. This photograph, taken in BR livery in September 1950, shows the attractive lines of the class before the later double chimneys were fitted. The tender is the post-war flush-sided design.

suburban services not being inaugurated until September 1949.

National priorities in the late 1940s concentrated on housing and other rebuilding schemes to make good the years of damage from bombing and to meet the aspirations of the returning servicemen for a home of their own to house themselves, their wives and the resulting 'baby bulge'. The Great Western was anxious to increase the provision of its own housing for staff, whose return from the forces was, in the main, not given any particular priority compared with other employees. Even before the end of the war large quantities of glass, tiles and slates were being moved into the worst bombed areas to start the housing repairs. It was necessary to regulate the flow of slate wagons particularly, so that they could be unloaded promptly and returned to the quarries so they could maintain their production.

From the railways' point of view, the post-war shortages represented only one of the problems they had to face, as the election in July 1945 had returned a Labour Government to power with a manifesto promising a major programme of nationalisation which included that of the railways. As early as November 1945 they announced their intention to introduce the necessary legislation during the life of that Parliament, and the Act received the Royal Assent on 6 August 1947, with vesting day being fixed for the start of 1948. Against this general background, therefore, we must now consider the events of the last three years of the Great Western.

Motive Power

The construction of mixed-traffic locomotives had continued during the war, with Hawksworth introducing his modified Halls in 1941, which continued to be built in batches until 1944 and then again from 1947 onwards. By the summer of 1945 Swindon had built the first of the 1000 class of 4–6–0, later to become the Counties. They incorporated some of the design features introduced in the Halls, but included a number of new developments. The first appeared with a double chimney, a feature which was fitted to the whole class much later, but of a modified design which was nothing like as attractive as the first version or the single variety. Continuous splashers were fitted over the driving wheels, which were 6 ft 3 in in diameter, intermediate in size between those of the Halls and Kings. The boiler operated at a pressure of 280 lb per sq in, higher even than that of the Kings; a decade later it was reduced to 250 lb per sq in in the interests of lower maintenance costs. Another visual difference was the introduction of a new design of 4,000-gallon tender, retaining the same profile as the earlier design, but flush-sided and involving the extensive use of welding. The class was a handsome addition to the Great Western stable, particularly as its appearance marked the return

of the green lined-out livery, but, like any powerful two-cylinder design, a County was a somewhat rougher-riding machine compared with the four-cylinder variety. Naming began in the spring of the following year, and at the same time names started to be given to the anonymous wartime-built modified Halls numbered 6916 to 6970.

The Counties were mixed-traffic designs, and as such were to receive British Railways lined black livery, but in 1946 Swindon started to build a further batch of Castles which were quite definitely express passenger designs. The first of these were no 5098 'Clifford Castle', and no 5099 'Compton Castle', the latter being used to haul the Royal Train to Oxford five months later, looking absolutely immaculate. The visit was to enable the King and Queen to open the New Bodleian Library, but the visit to the University did not conclude until after nine that evening. Between the arrival and departure times of the Royal Train, the extensive decorations at Oxford station were transferred from the down to the up side, and I was one of the small party on the down platform that watched the train depart for Paddington at 9.35. Once the Royal party had made its farewells, and boarded the train, 'Compton Castle' made one of the most silent starts I have ever observed with a steam locomotive, just gliding out of the station, in marked contrast to the usual explosive exhaust beats of a typical Great Western departure. With a booking of eighty-five minutes for the sixty-three miles to Paddington, however, there was no need to hurry. It is worth recording that at the time of this visit, no less than six Great Western railwaymen were serving on the Oxford City Council, one of them as Mayor.

Having exhausted the 50XX series with the construction of the first two new Castles, the remainder were numbered in the 70XX series. No 7000 itself was named 'Viscount Portal' after

BBC Hulton Picture Library

24. 'Garth Hall', the first of the GWR's mixed-traffic locomotives to be fitted for oil burning. The locomotive was later renumbered from 5955 to 3950 to record the changed fuel system used. A fire extinguisher can be seen on the footsteps to the cab, and the sliding shutters on the cab windows are also visible. These were a standard feature on all GWR oil-fired locomotives.

the Chairman of the company. The new locomotives all had three-row superheaters, which increased the temperature of the steam entering the cylinders from 525° to 580°F (approximately 275°–305°C), and from no 7000 onwards this was combined with the use of mechanical lubricators for the cylinders in place of the displacement variety. As will be discussed at a later stage, the Great Western, having been the first railway to introduce superheating in Britain, had lagged somewhat in the increase in temperature sought for compared with other railways, and these moves represented a welcome step forward after a long period of stagnation.

Swindon was also active in the construction of other new locomotives during this period. After a gap of four years more of Collett's 0–6–0 tender locomotives were built from October 1944 onwards, seventy being constructed before the last two came out in British Railways' days

25. Just before Nationalisation the GWR ordered two gas-turbine locomotives. The first was built in Switzerland and carried the number 18000. Over 30 years later the raised numerals can still be seen on the side of the locomotive, standing outside the Arsenal test plant in Vienna, although the bauxite livery now carried is very different from the black one used in Britain, when it was nicknamed 'Kerosene Castle'. In its days as a mobile testing unit for the Union Internationale des Chemins de Fer, it acquired the rather more romantic name 'Elisabella', which can be seen painted on the front of the cab.

in January 1948. Starting with no 4140 in August 1946 some more large Prairie tanks of the 41XX class were completed at Swindon, construction continuing until the end of 1949. Building of the large pannier 0–6–0T shunters continued throughout the war and went on until the end of 1950. There were only ten in the 1947 batch, however, compared with the twenty-eight con-

structed in the previous year and forty-three in 1945.

Early in 1947 a totally new design of 0–6–0 tank locomotive was produced at Swindon, combining for the first time two of the GWR's distinctive features – pannier tanks and a taper boiler. These were the 94XX class, and, while intended mainly for shunting work, also found themselves working branch line trains. They became a common sight at Paddington, standing at the buffer stops having brought the empty stock for down trains into the terminus. Only the first ten of the class were superheated, and these were the only ones built by the GWR. Construction of the unsuperheated versions commenced in earnest in 1950 under BR auspices, until the class totalled 210, all the others being constructed by private builders for service on the Western Region. No 9400 itself is in the National Collection and is on view to the public in the Great Western Railway Museum at Swindon. The cabs were taken out to the full width of the GWR loading gauge, which necessitated the footsteps being recessed into the side of the bunker. Copper-capped chimneys were fitted.

As already mentioned, the Great Western carried out a major programme of oil-firing in the years following the war, to try and overcome the shortage of coal and its rising price. Between 1945 and 1947 twenty 2–8–0s were converted and eventually renumbered in the 48XX series to differentiate them from the rest. The Anglo-Iranian Oil Company assisted Swindon with the conversion, which used a special burner at the front of the firebox. Steam was used for atomising purposes as well as keeping the heavy fuel mobile enough to flow by gravity to the burner from the rectangular tank in what was originally the coal-space on the tender. Following the success of these heavy freight locomotives, conversion of one of the Halls was carried out in June 1946. This was 'Garth Hall' and in the following year another ten were converted. Again they were given new numbers, this time in the 39XX series. Finally, it was the turn of the Castles and five of them were adapted to run on oil in 1946 and 1947, but had all been reconverted to coal firing by the end of 1948.

In the main the experiments were successful, but my only personal experience behind an oil-burner was not exactly sparkling. 'Rhuddlan Castle' was in charge of a thirteen-coach West of England express via Bristol one day in March 1947, and, after catching the train at Didcot, it was only the descent of Dauntsey incline that got the speed above 50 mph for the first time. The whole scheme was sufficiently promising, however, to prompt the Government to sponsor

a large-scale conversion scheme on all the railways to help overcome the coal shortages. It was proposed to convert 1,200 locomotives to save a million tons a year. A total of ninety-three locomotives was actually altered, including the Great Western's thirty-six, but by 1947 the supply of sufficient oil fuel could not be guaranteed, and the scheme was halted. Early in 1948 the British Transport Commission decided that the additional cost of nearly £300,000 a year for using oil fuel was not then justified, and the locomotives were switched back to coal. The equipment and fuelling installations were maintained for some years thereafter in case of emergencies.

While the other three railway companies were all considering main-line diesel-electric locomotives during the post-war years, the GWR went one better and ordered one powered by a gas-turbine. Britain was at the time very proud of Sir Geoffrey Whittle's invention of the aircraft jet engine, and the project caught the national interest. Reference was made to the plans at the Great Western Annual Meeting in March 1946, and it was decided to obtain two such locomotives. The first to be ordered was built in Switzerland, where a similar smaller locomotive was already operating. It had a brake horsepower of 2,500, but a more powerful one was then offered by the British firm of Metropolitan Vickers, with a nominal output of 3,000 horsepower. Both were to operate extensively on the Western Region of British Railways from 1950 onwards, the Metrovick machine working some formidable loads over the South Devon banks on test runs. Like all gas-turbine prime movers that operate at or near sea level, their high fuel consumptions under part-load conditions made them expensive to operate and they were ultimately withdrawn. The British-built locomotive, no 18100, was subsequently converted to a 25kV straight-electric for driver training purposes on the Crewe-Manchester line, while the earlier one was returned to Switzerland. This was no 18000, which had acquired the nickname 'Kerosene Castle'. Some time later, under UIC auspices, it was converted to a test vehicle, being stripped of its gas turbine. At the time of writing it stands on an isolated length of track outside the Arsenal test station in Vienna, still with its original number on the cab-side.

Rolling Stock

The shortages of the post-war period were to have a marked effect on the construction of new carriages at Swindon in the late 1940s. By the autumn of 1944 plans had been prepared for the new generation of Hawksworth vehicles, and the 1946 construction programme envisaged the works turning out 260 of the new designs at the rate of five a week, but even that proved optimistic. The new designs were very different from their predecessors, but not all the new features were to go into full-scale production. Externally the sides were vertical except for the taper just above the sole bar, but the roof-line had dipped ends, a characteristic that had long distinguished Gresley's coaches for the GNR and LNER, but which Thompson had just abandoned. Initially it was proposed to use fluorescent lighting inside the coaches, with 'Empire veneers' or Formica for the panelling. Neither was in the end used extensively in the production batches, but the interiors were nevertheless very attractive with oak veneer or enamelled hardboard. They were very comfortable vehicles to travel in from the point of view of the seating and also the ride. They incorporated the same general layouts as the pre-war vehicles, with four doors on each side, and, at sixty-four feet, were longer than the previous standard. A number of first-class sleepers was

planned as early as 1946, but the batch of four twelve-wheelers was not completed until 1951. During the same period many of the pre-war restaurant cars were modernised with new interior designs, while in 1946 an idea was announced for an 'Automat' buffet-car. Many hundreds of coin-operated compartments were to have been provided to sell food, cigarettes and even 'medical requisites'. The idea never materialised, although fifteen years later a much smaller version was provided for a time in standard BR vehicles used on the 'Cambrian Coast Express' between Shrewsbury and Aberystwyth.

Civil Engineering

In the main the efforts of the civil engineer and his department in the years 1945–1947 were concentrated on making good the wear and tear of six years of war, but they were able to start using some of the mechanical aids that had become commonplace in support of the Allied armed forces. In the autumn of 1946 a special engineers' demonstration train toured the GWR, being shown to some 2,500 members of the staff at eight different locations. In pre-war days track re-laying had been, quite literally, a manual job, but 1946 saw not only the introduction of prefabricated track panels but the experimental trials of flat-bottom track. The first section was laid on the up main between Slough and Langley, and it was intended to install thirty-eight miles of this type of track before the end of that year. The renewal programme involved a total of 417 miles in 1946, compared with a wartime annual average of only 250, which had resulted in a back-log of six hundred miles by the end of 1945.

However, the railways generally were looking forward to major new capital works after the

66

war. With the need to rebuild our devastated cities, town-planning had come to the fore, and the resulting involvement of planners in town and country was to have a marked effect on the country as a whole. Ideas were put forward at one time for new towns at White Waltham and Didcot, both of which would have involved the Great Western very considerably. One only has to consider the increased rail travel that has resulted in recent years from 'new towns' such as Peterborough, Stevenage and Milton Keynes to realise the effect these would have had on the GWR's system. As early as 1944 a committee had been appointed to consider the railways of London, and in their report in 1946 they put forward an extremely far-reaching series of proposals for new underground lines crossing the centre of the capital. Many of these were intended to take main-line stock, and it was proposed that there should be through running, for example, from Paddington via Charing Cross and Waterloo by a new line that resurfaced east of London Bridge on the Southern Railway's South Eastern Division. This was the only route that would have directly involved the GWR, and clearly would have required some form of motive power other than steam. It was accepted that 'under the most favourable conditions the whole scheme would take at least thirty years to complete'. Forty years on we are now actively considering reinstating one of the then-existing freight links (via Snow Hill), which was taken out of use in the interim.

Even in London, however, the Great Western was active in a number of new capital schemes during the post-war period. Work had begun before the war on the extension of the LPTB Central Line at both ends. As described in Part Two, the Great Western was involved in the construction work alongside their line to High Wycombe, but the start of the war prevented completion. Priority had been given to opening the extensions at the eastern end, but on 30 June 1947 the first stretch of the line built by the Great Western opened, from North Acton to Greenford, the continuation to Ruislip coming into use in November the following year. Although only used by Tube trains, the track was the property of the GWR until nationalisation, after which it passed to the London Transport Executive.

The Great Western was also active on its own account with some of the schemes resurrected from the Railways (Agreement) Act of 1935. They decided not to proceed with the Dawlish avoiding line described in Part Two, but were considering the possibility of a short length of quadruple track through Teignmouth, which would have enabled trains to call there without holding up the procession of expresses running 'block-to-block' on a summer Saturday. There was also talk of providing separate lines for the Southern Railway's trains between Cowley Bridge Junction and St David's station in Exeter, apparently without going back to the one-time plans for a flyover. Neither of these schemes went ahead and the Great Western's West of England lines were to become increasingly an operators' nightmare on summer Saturdays, as has been described so well by David St John Thomas and Simon Rocksborough Smith in their book on the subject. British Railways, like the Great Western, became locked-in to the problem of peak summer capacities, and it was the Beeching Report which highlighted the amount of stock retained for just a few journeys each year.

The Great Western also announced plans to lay extra tracks from Steventon to Wantage Road, and from Challow to Wootton Bassett, which would have given an eighty-three mile stretch of quadruple line, the longest in the country, running all the way from Paddington to where the Bristol and South Wales routes

26. The exterior of one of the Hawksworth post-war carriages for the GWR. This is a brake composite, and shows the post-Nationalisation suffix W to the number. The low ends to the roof are prominent.

British Rail Western Region

diverged, but this never fully materialised. In Wales some further work was carried out on one of the 1935 schemes. This was on the Porthcawl branch, which it was intended to double throughout. The seaside town was a popular resort for people from Swansea, and plans had been drawn up in pre-war days for various improvements. A double-line spur to permit through running from the west on to the branch at Pyle had been built before the war, but not connected, and as well as completing this, work started on the doubling of the section from Cornelly to Nottage. Many of the Great Western's post-war aspirations are set out in Christian Barman's book *Next Station*★. In it reference is made to the work between Cornelly and Nottage being in hand, but in the end it got no

further than the earth-moving stage before capital expenditure restrictions intervened. The new spur at Pyle, however, served a useful purpose in permitting the direct running of limestone trains as well as the through morning and evening residential services to and from Swansea, but the branch closed to passengers in 1963 and has now disappeared.

Up in North Wales the Butlin's holiday camp at Peny-y-Chain between Pwllheli and Criccieth had a new station built for it, ready for the reopening at Easter 1947, with double track extending to Afonwen, the junction between the GWR and LMS lines. Few at that time would have imagined that a Stanier Pacific would become one of the camp's attractions, or that regular coach trips would be run from it to take holidaymakers to the restored Festiniog Railway.

In 1946 the Great Western shareholders were asked to approve the submission of a Parlia-

★George Allen & Unwin, 1947.

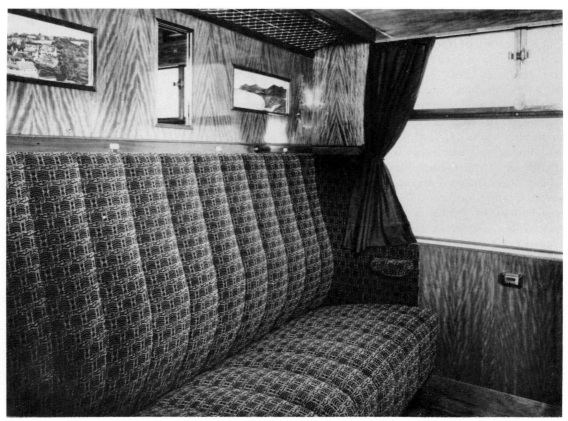

27. The interior of one of the third-class compartments of Hawksworth's post-war stock. The attractive modern styling is obvious, and the seats were every bit as comfy as they looked, although passengers were expected to sit four a side. Different-coloured upholstery was used to identify smoking and non-smoking compartments.

BBC Hulton Picture Library

mentary bill to build a new 1½-mile branch, together with the necessary marshalling yards, to serve the steel works being constructed at Margam by Guest Keen & Baldwins Iron & Steel Company, which was, in due course, to dominate the view from the GWR main line approaching Port Talbot from the east.

On the signalling side, one development was the installation of warning bell and telephone connections between certain airfield control towers and the nearby railway signalbox, for use if an aircraft should crash on the line. One wonders if this was prompted by the incident at White Waltham already recorded. During the war the LNER had introduced its own automatic warning system at some airfields, following a fatal accident. Their installations comprised trip wires along the side of the vulnerable length of track, which would be severed by a crashing aircraft and would switch on special colour-light signals to warn the drivers of approaching trains.

Train Services

The restoration of train services in the post-war years was very much a case of two steps forward and one step back. No sooner had it been possible to introduce some form of acceleration or a new facility than another crisis caused a change of plan. In December 1946, for example, numerous main-line and local services were withdrawn to conserve coal supplies, and, a month later, still further cuts were necessary. These moves were quite independent of the severe weather conditions that did not start until mid-January 1947. Even when the next winter's timetables came into operation in the following October, the services were some 10 per cent less than they had been a year earlier. At the same time there was a 16½ per cent fare increase, bringing the standard third-class single to 2.44d (1p) per mile, with monthly returns working out at 1.63d (⅔p). Cheap day fares and some other similar facilities had been reintroduced at the beginning of August 1946, which resulted in the GWR Stationery and Printing Department having to produce some four million new tickets at short notice.

The Travelling Post Office services between London and Penzance were reintroduced on 1 October 1945, the down train being waved off from Paddington by the Postmaster General. For the occasion some of the stock had been repainted in Great Western chocolate and cream livery, with 'Royal Mail' emblazoned on the side, the words being separated by the late-fee posting box and the royal cypher. On the other hand, the Great Western was deliberately slower in reintroducing restaurant cars than the other lines, who had brought theirs back into service on 1 October. In view of the heavy loadings on GWR main-line services at that time it was not felt desirable to force yet more people to stand, while the crowded corridors themselves would have made it difficult to call passengers to the cars for each sitting. The other companies withdrew their cars over the Christmas period that year, but when they were reintroduced on New Year's Eve the Great Western had its first fourteen trains duly equipped with this facility.

October 1947 saw the withdrawal of the Plymouth-Yealmpton service which had been reintroduced in 1941 after the Blitz in Plymouth, as referred to earlier, while some of the special services to ordnance factories were thinned out after the war as the demand for munitions tailed off. On the other hand, 1947 saw the reopening of the Vale of Rheidol narrow-gauge line from Aberystwyth to Devil's Bridge, the seasonal services over which had not been operated during the war.

On the freight side there were important services to be restarted. Express freight trains with vacuum braking were reintroduced in May 1945 between London and South Wales, to be followed progressively by similar services to other destinations, a total of sixty-eight being in operation by the end of the year. In the same period Swansea loaded a cargo of coal for export to Italy, the first since 1940. Even more welcome was the return of the banana traffic, banned since Christmas 1940. The Great Western had been closely involved with this, considerable quantities of fruit being distributed by them from Avonmouth Docks in the special steam-heated vans.

Docks and Marine Activities

As in other spheres of activity, 1945 marked only the start of the return to normality in the Great Western's docks and marine activities. Indeed the whole question of South Wales and its docks was one that had been seriously concerning the company even before the end of

28. The first-class saloon of a refurbished GWR restaurant car in November 1946. Rotatable tub chairs were provided, together with quite fancy ironwork supports for the tables. The long mirrors between the windows were decorated with flying birds and trees.

the war. Changed patterns of coal production and imports were likely to undermine seriously the prosperity of the area in the post-war period, and prior to 1939 the Great Western had relied heavily on the freight and passenger revenue from that part of the country, in spite of the

heavy holiday traffic to the West of England, which tended to receive a lot of the publicity. Numerous high-level visits were made by directors and officers of the GWR to the cities and towns along the north coast of the British Channel, emphasising the services the railway could offer and stressing the contributions all parties could jointly make to the future prosperity of the area. In the summer of 1946 General John C.H. Lee, the former commander of the US Supply Service in the European Theatre of Operations, visited Britain and toured various ports to pass on General Eisenhower's thanks for their work during the war. Great play was made of the contribution of the Great Western's South Wales installations which had handled nearly 4¾ million tons of American supplies from 1942 onwards. General Lee referred to the fact that the Bristol Channel ports had loaded no less than 78 per cent of the American loads after D-Day.

Although early steps were to be taken to repair the wartime bomb damage at the South Wales ports, the installations as a whole were to continue their downward trend in the post-war period, the total tonnage handled falling from 15.7 million tons in 1944 to 10.2 million in 1947. Many factors played their part in this. As we have already discussed in earlier volumes, the tidal pattern in the Bristol Channel and Severn Estuary necessitated locks at the entrances of the South Wales ports, which slowed down arrivals and departures, and caused complications with the steadily-increasing size of ships in the post-war period.

On the shipping side the Great Western's activities were rather more rewarding. Replacements were ordered for the 'St David' and 'St Patrick' that had been sunk during the war, and two fine vessels were built with the same names, the former being launched in February 1947. The new 'St Patrick' entered the water in the following May, carrying the pennant her predecessor had been flying when she was sunk in the Bristol Channel. However, while the 'St David' went into service across the Irish Sea in July of that year, the maiden voyage of the 'St Patrick' on the Channel Islands' service from Weymouth was not to take place until February 1948, although the 'St David' had undertaken trials on that service during the previous autumn. The ships were generally similar, with variations in their internal accommodation to meet the differing requirements of the Irish and Channel Island services.

The Channel Island services from Weymouth had restarted in September 1945 but only with the 'Roebuck' and 'Sambur', which were able to take a dozen passengers in addition to cargo and mails. They even started called once a week from June 1946 at Alderney, which was a new service destination for the Great Western. That island had been completely evacuated before the German invasion and was used by them as a huge prison camp, so post-war rehabilitation was particularly difficult after the evacuees had returned. It was in June 1946, however, that normal passenger services to and from Jersey and Guernsey restarted when the 'St Helier' re-entered service after a refit. Appearing in proper railway colours, her first voyage was greeted with salutes from warships of the Home Fleet at Portland, while two commemorative plaques had been fitted to record her wartime exploits. The 'St Julien' returned to the service in November, and between them they handled 122,000 passengers in the following year, which was nearly 10 per cent up on the best pre-war figure, achieved in 1938. With foreign-travel allowances severely restricted, the Channel Islands became a popular holiday destination, and would-be passengers queued at Paddington for sailing tickets.

The Fishguard-Waterford services restarted in July 1945, but the 'St Andrew' was still not available for the Fishguard-Rosslare service until the following year, being hard at work as a troop transport. The need for her hospital facilities had fortunately ceased. The first post-war call of a passenger liner in Plymouth Sound also took place in the summer of 1945, but this operation was never to become as extensive as it had been in pre-war days. The tender 'Sir Francis Drake' did not return to this duty, being sold by the GWR soon after her return from war service, but 'Sir Richard Grenville' was still there when the service ceased at the end of October 1963. One somewhat unusual call at Plymouth was that of the United States cruiser 'Augusta' in August 1945, with President Truman aboard. The King travelled to Plymouth by Royal Train and there were formal exchange visits aboard the American vessel and HMS 'Renown'. Though it was no fault of the GWR, this particular incident was not too well received in Britain, many people taking the view that the American head of state ought at least to have landed in Britain, even if he could not manage to visit London.

Road Transport

Although the Great Western's road fleet did not increase in size during the war, it was extensively employed, and, in the light of this experience, there were clearly advantages to be gained in the further integration of road and rail goods activities at a local level. The handling of small consignments was further concentrated in a very limited number of zones. Taking the South Wales area as an example, the forty-six stations that dealt with this type of business were further cut to just eleven.

On the passenger side, the railway's interests continued to be exploited through their associated omnibus and coach companies. As will be

29. No 5056 'Usk Castle' leaving Reading on an ATC test run on October 5th 1947. Behind the Dynamometer Car are two of the pre-war Centenary Stock. The run was to demonstrate that the special ATC indication for Double-Yellow signals worked at high speeds.

M. W. Earley Collection, National Railway Museum, York

seen in the subsequent section dealing with finance, the effect of petrol rationing made the Great Western's holdings very profitable indeed.

It must not be forgotten that the Great Western still operated many horse-drawn vehicles during its final years. Although its stock of horses had declined between 1939 and 1945 by 30 per cent from the pre-war figure of 1,584, there were still a lot at work, while 1 se for shunting purposes remained fairly constant in the range of twenty to twenty-four. In its final year of operation the GWR even acquired one extra horse wagon or cart to bring their total to 2,357, while harness competitions were still a feature of the annual staff calendar.

30. Work on the Western extension of the LPTB Central Line recommenced early in 1946, and the publicity of the time referred to the fact that 'most of the men now engaged on the work have never before worked on a railway. They were chosen because they are tough, used to outdoor work, and keen on the job.' The caption went on to refer to the train roaring past on the old line, but with due respect to the single auto trailer, this is a somewhat optimistic description of a Pannier tank's performance.

Hotels and Refreshment Rooms

As part of its post-war plans, the Great Western was anxious to extend its hotel operations. Reference was made in Part Two to the new plans for Looe before the war. Although there was no more discussion about the new branch line from St Germans, the hotel was extensively referred to in the book *Next Station*. Changed civic plans for the centre of Birmingham rendered the pre-war plans for a new business hotel at Snow Hill out of date, and that project was not revived. However, two new hotels were being actively considered in 1947 as part of the post-war boost to South Wales. Each was to have about 200 bedrooms, provided with private bathrooms, and an artist's impression of the one at Swansea was included in *Next Station*. A sun-terrace over the entrance hall would have provided space for visitors to sit and look across the sea towards Mumbles. Eventually, neither was built, nor was the smaller one, with seventy bedrooms, planned for Swindon.

If the Great Western's expansion plans at this time were to be thwarted, their four existing hotels returned as quickly as circumstances permitted to something nearer their pre-war standard. The Manor House Hotel at Moretonhampstead was derequisitioned and it reopened in October 1946, while the service personnel who had occupied the larger part of the Fishguard Bay Hotel had already left. At Paddington renovations to the wartime fire damage on one floor of the Great Western Royal Hotel were put in hand, while the Tregenna Castle's herd of Jersey cattle returned to the home farm, and there were hopes that Cornish clotted cream would soon be allowed to re-appear on the tea tables. Suitably festive events were also arranged for Christmas and the New Year.

An extensive review was undertaken of the railway's refreshment rooms at stations, which had been called on to provide sustenance for so many additional travellers during the war years. Mention has already been made of the wartime introduction of staff canteens, and by November 1946 the Great Western had completed its seventy-fifth such facility. It was opened at Swansea by the Company's Chairman and the General Secretary of the NUR, and also served as a social club, being run by 'a committee of employees drawn from all departments'.

Air Services

Although the Great Western had long-ceased its direct involvement in air services, it nevertheless had an interest in the resumption of the Channel Island operations from Croydon in 1945 by Jersey Airways. By the following summer over 180 services a week were being worked, the 'Dragon Rapides' being supplemented first by 'Dakotas' and then by the new Bristol 'Way-farer', better known in its subsequent 'Freighter' version with its car-carrying capabilities. The Labour Government had, in November 1945, announced its plans to set up British European Airways, which would also operate all scheduled internal services in Britain, and the railways' involvement was thereby to cease, although in the transitional period they and their associated airlines acted as agents for the new corporation.

Financial Results

In the earlier parts of this book we have considered the Great Western Railways' financial performance relative to those of the other groups. Presenting similar figures during and after World War II gives a picture that is to a large degree distorted, because, when the Government took over the operation of the railways in the autumn of 1939 the whole question of railway finance became the subject of discussions with the Treasury. After an interim arrangement for 1940, from 1 January 1941 until at least a year after the end of hostilities, the Government undertook to meet the running costs of the railways and keep the total revenue, allocating them, as a whole, the sum of just over £43 million per year. This was to be divided between the four main-line companies and the London Passenger Transport Board. The Great

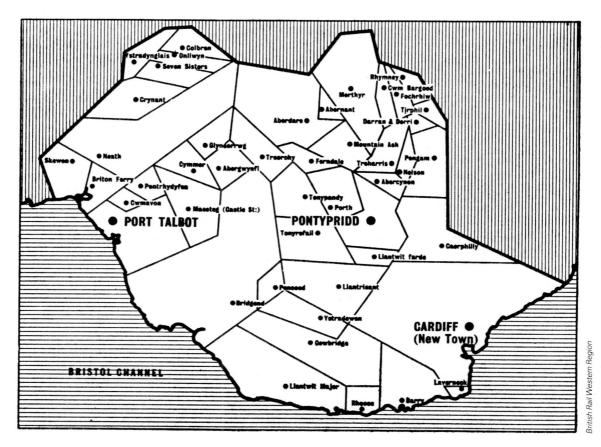

British Rail Western Region

Western's share of this net revenue was £6,670,603, but it still retained certain other sources of income which were over and above that coming from the Government. It was from the overall net revenue that interest and dividends were paid, with a balance being carried forward from year to year. In 1946 there was a profit of nearly a quarter of a million pounds on the realisation of investments, which was added to the total available for distribution to the shareholders. With the pending nationalisation of the railways the same system was continued through to 1947, but the net revenue available actually increased slightly from year to year, as shown by the following figures.

Table 7 GREAT WESTERN NET REVENUE

Year	Total Net Revenue (£)
1939	6,607,324
1940	6,793,987
1941	6,931,767
1942	6,932,746
1943	6,939,982
1944	6,940,129
1945	6,943,585
1946	7,467,390★
1947	7,539,771

★ Plus £245,074 profit on realisation of investments
Source: GWR Annual Reports

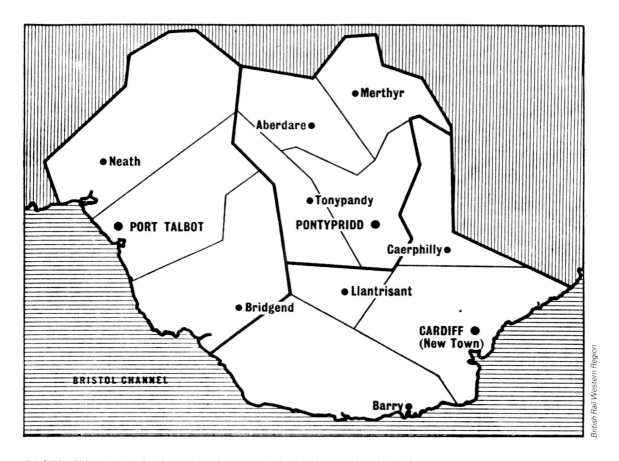

31. & 32. Although there had been a drastic reorganisation of the general goods traffic arrangements between the wars, even greater changes took place in 1946. In the South Wales area 46 different delivery areas were amalgamated into just 11, grouped into three zones, each with its own railhead (shown in capitals).

This modest increase was due very largely to the increased dividends the company received on their investments in associated undertakings such as the bus services, the Hay's Wharf Cartage Company and the Penarth Pontoon, Slipway & Ship Repairing Company. In 1941 the total received on this account was £256,226 but had increased to £825,294 in 1947. These investments had become very profitable indeed by this stage, as shown in Table 8, which, in the case of the omnibus companies, can be com-

pared with those for 1939 which were given in Volume 2. The nominal value of the Great Western's holdings in the associated bus companies was unchanged during this period, but the profitability of the undertakings increased very considerably, although the returns varied very appreciably from one to another. The holding in the Hay's Wharf Cartage Company increased very considerably, however, and percentage profitability was up by a factor of nearly three between 1939 and 1947. These figures, and

77

Table 8 GWR'S INTEREST AND DIVIDENDS FROM INVESTMENTS
IN OTHER UNDERTAKINGS – 1947

Name of undertaking	Investment (£)	Interest (£)	Dividends (%)
Associated Bus Companies			
Birmingham & Midland Motor Omnibus Co Ltd	411,500	201,600	49.0
City of Oxford Motor Services Ltd	123,868	51,364	41.5
Crosville Motor Services Ltd	148,212	25,536	17.2
Devon General Omnibus & Touring Co Ltd	62,954	22,504	35.8
Thames Valley Traction Co Ltd	93,710	36,400	38.8
Western National Omnibus Co Ltd	1,263,378	187,636	14.9
Western Welsh Omnibus Co Ltd	196,520	59,977	30.5
Other Companies			
Hays Wharf Cartage Co Ltd	795,808	238,888	30.0
Penarth Pontoon, Slipway & Ship Repairing Co Ltd	37,750[1]	1,389	3.7

1   Figure assumed as it is not quoted in the Annual Report
Source: GWR Annual Report

those for the other railways, amply vindicate the policy adopted during the inter-war period of making investments in road transport activities. All this was to change, of course, after nationalisation, with the formation of separate executives for bus and road haulage activities as operating arms of the British Transport Commission.

As discussed in Volume 2, the dividend on the Great Western's ordinary shares had been cut to ½ per cent in 1938 as a political gesture in the Square Deal campaign, but Table 9 shows how the holder of GWR ordinary shares fared during the last nine years of the company's existence. Included in the table are the corresponding dividends on the ordinary shares of the other three main-line railways, and it will be seen that throughout the period the Great Western maintained a better rate of interest than the other companies achieved. This was in spite of government control of the railways, and thus might at first reading appear to be somewhat surprising. However, when the different companies arrived at their shares of the Government's

annual payments, the proportions each received was coloured by their pre-war performance, when, as we saw, the Great Western had managed to produce higher dividends than the others.

Under the 1947 Transport Act, the balance on the net revenue account carried forward at the beginning of 1946 passed in due course to the British Transport Commission, but when the Great Western was formally wound up the rest of the accumulated net revenue was available to be distributed to the ordinary shareholders. An interim dividend of 2 per cent had been paid in the summer of 1947, and the recommendations for the final distribution were submitted '. . . to the Proprietors at a General Meeting to be held at the Great Western Royal Hotel, Paddington Station, on Friday, the 5th day of March, 1948, at 12.00 noon'. It was proposed that the final dividend should be 5.282158 per cent, which, by going to six places of decimals, neatly ensured that the whole of the balance available was distributed to the ordinary shareholders. The other three main-line companies did not manage

Table 9 RAILWAY DIVIDENDS

Year	GWR	LMS	LNER		SR	
			Preferred	*Deferred*	*Preferred*	*Deferred*
1939	3½	1½	nil	nil	5	1¼
1940	4	1½	nil	nil	5	1¼
1941	4	2	nil	nil	5	1¾
1942	4½	2½	nil	nil	5	1¾
1943	4½	2½	nil	nil	5	2
1944	4½	2½	nil	nil	5	2
1945	5	4	nil	nil	5	2
1946	5	2¾	nil	nil	5	2¾
1947[3]	7.282158	4.895625[1]	0.958[2]	nil	5	4⅙

Percentage Dividends on Ordinary Shares

1   Quoted in the Annual Report as £4 : 17s : 10¹⁹⁄₂₀d
2   Quoted in Annual Report as 19s 2d
3   Income tax on the 1947 dividends was at the rate of 45 per cent
Source: Company Annual Reports

33. The 'Saint Patrick' at Weymouth in June 1954, still sporting GWR livery, and with the railway company's coat-of-arms on the bows.

Locomotive Club of Great Britain/Ken Nunn Collection

it anything like so well, although the LMS, by declaring their final dividend as £4:17s:10¹⁹/₂₀d, got nearest, with a balance of £49 being handed over to the British Transport Commission. The corresponding figures for the LNER and SR were £224 and £411.

The problems of obtaining allocations of manpower and materials during World War II and immediately afterwards meant that the railways were unable to carry out as much maintenance as they would have wished, and it was accepted that money should be put aside to meet the deferred work. The sums involved were very considerable indeed, and by 1947 the total for the four main-line railways, together with the LPTB amounted to nearly £148 million, the figure for the GWR being £18,045,196. Each of the five organisations had a Trust Fund set up under the Railway Control Agreement, with one railway nominee and trustee, and one from the Government. This money was represented in the balance sheets as an asset, but was of course not available to the shareholders and passed to the British Transport Commission on 1 January 1948 with the railways' physical assets. One assumes, however, that the existence of these financial assets was carefully referred to in the course of negotiations on the amounts of government stock that were to be exchanged for that of the railway companies following nationalisation. We will be discussing at a later stage the way the proprietors of the GWR fared under the 1947 Transport Act.

Before that is done it is appropriate to consider in more detail how the railways themselves did financially under government control from 1939 onwards. As we have seen, the five organisations as a whole received a net revenue of about £43 million each year, which was, of course, a great deal less than the railways were actually achieving during these years. In 1943 alone, the real net revenue amounted to £105,568,000, and over the five years 1940–1944 the total came to nearly £393 million, of which the railways were allowed to retain £215 million. The five maintenance Trust Funds in 1947 only totalled some £148 million. So, even without including the surpluses received by the Government for the years 1945–47, the railways as a whole had lost some £30 million, in addition to the sums paid into the Trust Funds which they were never actually to receive. Ordinary companies during the war years were subject to an Excess Profits Tax, but it would be an extremely difficult task to estimate whether the proportion of the railways' income retained by the Government during this period represented a higher or lower proportion than it did generally in private industry.

3
Nationalisation

Five minutes after Big Ben had struck to mark the start of 1948, 'Usk Castle' left for Birkenhead with the first British Railways' train to leave Paddington. The assets of the Great Western Railway had formally been invested in the British Transport Commission as from 1 January, and it is worth considering what had

Table 10 ASSETS OF THE GWR VESTED IN THE BRITISH TRANSPORT COMMISSION ON 1 JANUARY 1948

Nominal capital authorised	£175,021,626
Capital created	£167,959,878
Expenditure on capital account	£189,992,856
Subscriptions to other undertakings	£4,961,795

Mileage of lines open for traffic
Route mileage	3737 miles 15 chains
Mileage of running lines	6577 miles 39 chains
Total track miles, including sidings	9244 miles 46 chains

Locomotives	Number	3857
	Weight	200,489 tons
	Miles run	92,013,683
Diesel railcars		37
Coaching vehicles		8,368
Wagons		87,403
Service vehicles		8,903
Motor road vehicles		2,682
Horse wagons and carts		2,357

Miscellaneous	1,849
Horses for road vehicles	1,126
Horses for shunting	22

Canals	Number owned	
	wholly or jointly	10
	Total length	208 miles 41 chains

Docks, harbours and wharves
Number owned, wholly or jointly or leased	16
Total length of quays	164,535 feet

Steamboats
Number owned	9
Number worked	11

Hotels
Number owned and worked	3
Number owned but not worked	2
Number worked but not owned	1

Land not forming part of the railway or stations
Agricultural land	3665 acres
Urban and suburban land	1821 acres

Houses
Labouring class dwellings	208
Houses and cottages for company's servants	2,259
Other houses and cottages	1,364
Advances to building societies and staff for housing	£737,824

Staff employed (on March 29, 1947)	113,601

Source: GWR Annual Report

34. Although their dimensions prevented them from operating everywhere, the GWR designs took part extensively in the Locomotive Exchanges of 1948. In this photograph, no 6990 'Witherslack Hall' arrives at Marylebone with a train from Manchester via Woodhead. This was one of the familiarisation trips without the dynamometer car. The locomotive was named after the home of the Hon. Oliver Stanley at Grange-over-Sands in Westmoreland (as it then was), a reminder that the GWR went well outside its own system when naming the Halls.

been built up over the 113 years since the original Act of Parliament had been passed. Table 10 lists some of them, and even by today's standards, after thirty-seven years of inflation, the financial totals are large. BR's 1982 total of freight vehicles was under 72,000, some 18 per cent less than GWR's, even if the modern fleet of coaching vehicles numbered about twice as many. It is not meaningful to compare diesel or electric traction with steam locomotives, but it is worth recording that British Railways' route mileage in 1982 was 10,706, less than three times that of the GWR.

It is interesting to look back and see how the shareholders of the Great Western Railway fared financially as a result of nationalisation. By way of compensation the Treasury issued British Transport 3 per cent guaranteed stock, redeem-

35. Shortly after Nationalisation some of the GWR locomotives appeared with the wording 'British Railways' on their tenders, painted in traditional GWR lettering. No 7008 'Swansea Castle' hauls a through train of Southern stock past Bentley Heath in September 1948. This was one of the high-superheat locomotives built after the war, and had a flush-sided tender.

Millbrook House Collection/C. F. Oldham

Table 11   EXCHANGE RATES FOR 3 PER CENT BRITISH TRANSPORT STOCK

GWR stock	*Amount of British Transport 3 per cent stock per £1 nominal*		*Equivalent new interest rate for £1 nominal*	*1947 yield based on price at 30 December 1947*
	(£/shillings/pence)	*(£p)*★	*(per cent)*	*(per cent)*†
2½ per cent debenture	19s : 1⅕d	£0.955	2.87	2.76
4 per cent debenture	£1 : 5s : 7¹³⁄₂₀d	£1.282	3.85	3.24
4¼ per cent debenture	£1 : 5s : 8¹⁷⁄₂₀d	£1.287	3.86	3.44
4½ per cent debenture	£1 : 6s : 0⁹⁄₁₀d	£1.304	3.91	3.59
5 per cent debenture	£1 : 8s : 5⁷⁄₁₀d	£1.424	4.27	3.64
5 per cent rent charge	£1 : 7s : 11¼d	£1.397	4.19	3.72
5 per cent consolidated guaranteed	£1 : 7s : 4⅘d	£1.370	4.11	3.77
5 per cent consolidated preference	£1 : 5s : 0⁹⁄₂₀d	£1.252	3.76	4.15
5 per cent redeemable preference (1950)	£1 : 1s : 3⅗d	£1.065	3.20	4.88
Consolidated ordinary	11s : 9¾d	£0.591	1.77	12.78

★ Rounded to three decimal places
† Rounded to two decimal places
Source: Railway Gazette, 9 January 1948

able in 1978–88, which was exchanged for the various different holdings in the railways whose assets had already passed into the hands of the British Transport Commission. There were ten different classes of GWR stock, and the exchange rates for each of these, as announced on 2 January 1948, are given in Table 11. It will be seen that, with the solitary exception of the 2½ per cent debentures, all classes of fixed interest stock received a lower rate of interest after the exchange. When allowance is made, however, for the prior Stock Exchange quotations for the different fixed-interest securities, it will be seen that the new rates of interest were somewhat higher in each case, indicating that investors on the Stock Exchange had partially discounted the exchange rate, which turned out to be somewhat higher than the current market price.

As we saw in the previous chapter, the final general meetings of the railway companies in March 1948 cleared the outstanding balances on their net revenue accounts, and the resulting rates of dividend on the ordinary shares for 1947 were somewhat exceptional. In view of this it is better to compare the fortunes of the ordinary Great Western shareholder with his opposite number in the other main-line companies on the basis of the 1946 dividends. These figures are given in Table 12. A comparison of Columns 1 and 3 shows that from a capital point of view, the shareholders received a slightly greater value of British Transport stock than they had owned at market value in the old companies. However it should be remembered that the new stock had dipped below 95 on the Stock Exchange before six months had elapsed. As far as interest was concerned, in every case the new yield, based on the conversion rate and the Stock Exchange prices at the end of 1947, worked out at 3.1 per cent, which was appreciably down on what the yield had been a year earlier, except in the case of the LNER which had not succeeded in paying a dividend on either class of its ordinary shares since 1937.

These were the hard finances of nationalisation, but initially the railways continued as they had done before, although the railway shareholder and railway director became extinct as far as the main line companies were concerned, but we shall see in the following chapter how the Great Western's traditions lived on in the years that followed the traumatic changes of 1 January 1948.

Table 12   EXCHANGE RATES AND YIELDS ON ORDINARY SHARES

Railway company		Stock Exchange price on 30/12/47 (per cent ex dividend)	Amount of BT 3 per cent stock per £1 nominal (shillings/pence)	(p)*	1946 dividend yield on price at 30/12/46 (per cent)*	Equivalent yield of new BT 3 per cent stock (per cent)*
GWR		57	11s 9¾d	59.1	8.8	3.1
LMSR		28½	5s 10⅘d	29.5	9.6	3.1
LNER	preferred	7	1s 5¹¹⁄₂₀d	7.3	nil	3.1
	deferred	3½	8⁷⁄₁₀d	3.6	nil	3.1
SR	preferred	75	15s 6³⁄₁₀d	77.6	6.7	3.1
	deferred	23½	4s 9⅗d	24.0	11.8	3.1

* Rounded to one decimal place
Source: *Railway Gazette* 2, 9 January 1948 Company Annual Reports

4
The Tradition Lives On

An organisation the size of the Great Western, which could trace its history over a period of no less than 113 years, was unlikely to change overnight, even after such a profound upset as nationalisation. Initially the former private railway company became the Western Region of British Railways, with Keith Grand, the former Assistant General Manager, as Chief Regional Officer. (Managing seemed to be a naughty word in the public sector in those days.) Clearly there were bound to be changes in a nationalised railway system, as new equipment and practices were introduced, boundaries were redrawn, and staff came and went on a country-wide basis for the first time. The Great Western tradition nevertheless lived on, and in this chapter I want briefly to review some of the significant features of British Railways' history in which the traditions of Paddington or Swindon played an important part. The influence might have been greater still had not Sir James Milne declined the Chairmanship of the Railway Executive because of outside interests.

Great Western signalling had long since standardised on the lower-quadrant semaphore variety, sited so they could be seen from where the drivers stood on the right-hand side of their footplates. All the other companies had introduced upper-quadrants between the wars, and when regional boundaries changed, signals of GWR design at times replaced the upper-quadrant variety originating from another company. On the Western Region itself there was some difficulty with the new standard classes of locomotive, which were designed for left-hand drive, and the difficulty of sighting signals from the footplate of a Britannia class Pacific was partly responsible for a serious derailment at Milton in 1955.

The Great Western had pioneered the use of cab signalling, known by them as ATC or Automatic Train Control. In spite of many Ministry of Transport recommendations for its use elsewhere, neither the other companies nor the Railway Executive had sanctioned widespread adoption of any such system. Following the war, an improved version of the Great Western system had been developed which was capable of giving different cab indications for double-yellow and single-yellow aspects, but work by the new Railway Executive continued slowly on a system that did not rely on actual contact between a shoe on the locomotive and a ramp between the rails. Quite apart from the safety aspects, the use of ATC greatly facilitated train-running in fog which, in those days before the introduction of smokeless zones, was much more common and severe in the vicinity of large towns. It was the double collision at Harrow & Wealdstone in October 1952 which gave the

36. One of the taper-boiler 0—6—0 Pannier tanks, no 8488, approaches Hatherley Junction, Cheltenham with a 5-coach train in 1952. This was one of the class built after Nationalisation by Robert Stephenson & Hawthorns Ltd. It has a BR smokebox numberplate, but the cab-side one was of GWR pattern, whereas locomotives from the other Groups had to be content with painted numerals. The signal gantry was put up when the line was quadrupled during the war, as described in chapter 1. All six distants, as well as the five stop signals are provided with position indicators to Hatherley Junction signalbox.

stimulus for the more widespread introduction of the Automatic Warning System, or AWS, which is now such a familiar feature of our main lines. In the fullness of time, the standard magnetic system was to replace the GWR's shoe and ramp version which had contributed so much to its safety record since 1905.

There was one other signalling matter where Great Western practice came into early conflict with the new British Railways' standards. This concerned the use of distant signals with temporary speed restrictions. Whenever a temporary speed restriction with its regulation signs was introduced, the GWR signalman in the box concerned would place a collar on the lever of the appropriate distant signal, which prevented it being pulled off until the track work was completed and normal running resumed. Elsewhere it was considered that the publication of the details in the weekly or fortnightly notices, coupled with the standard warning boards, was sufficient for the drivers, and after an appreciable degree of protest the signalmen on the Western Region had to follow suit. In retrospect it seems surprising that the change was made in that particular direction, bearing in mind the fact that warning boards for temporary speed restriction are now accompanied by their own AWS warning magnet, while, under the Approach Control system, colour-light signals remain obstinately at caution or danger as a train approaches a junction set for a low-speed diverging route. Only when the track circuits detect that the train is close enough to the red signal do they permit it to clear, the driver having thus been forced to reduce his speed to something comparable to that permitted over the junction. Generally speaking, however, the Western Region signalling rules were sufficiently different to result in the survival of their own version of the block regulations until the new version of the British Railways rule book was introduced as late as 1972.

Soon after nationalisation it was decided to hold a series of interchange trials between various different classes of locomotive from the four grouping companies, plus the wartime Austerities. Today we are used to our diesel motive power wandering all over the country, but the 1948 exchanges were a considerable innovation, and there was great rivalry between supporters of the different companies, professional and amateur alike. The more liberal GWR loading gauge prevented their locomotives wandering as widely as most, and when the results were published in 1950, Great Western supporters were somewhat disappointed with the showing of the Swindon designs. On both the Eastern and Western Regions, the Kings were well down the efficiency league tables. On their own routes the coal consumption per drawbar horsepower hour was the highest of the five classes tested, while between King's Cross and Leeds only the Southern Region's Merchant Navy locomotives turned in a worse result. The Halls came third on the list in each case, but the 28XX heavy freight locomotives were somewhat better. These results became apparent to Swindon immediately after the mains tests were complete, and as a result a further series of trials was run in the Western Region alone, with their own competing designs operating on the Welsh coal which they normally used, rather than the other varieties specified for the main trials. The results of these additional tests put the Hall and the 28XX at the top of their respective leagues on the Western Region routes, the latter achieving the lowest consumption by a considerable margin of any locomotive in the whole series. While the performance of the Kings improved on Welsh coal, one of the high-superheat locomotives was also tested, and this achieved the best consumption of any express locomotive tested on the Western Region. As already mentioned, the degree of superheating used on

Swindon designs had lagged behind the optimum and the results of these and other tests were to bring about major changes in the Kings and Castles in the years that followed. Four-row superheaters were adopted, together with double chimneys, which improved their performance considerably, even though the appearance of the locomotives suffered in consequence.

Swindon had long pioneered good smokebox design, and in the years following nationalisation they were to extend their researches in the subject. The results provided the design data which enabled the steaming capacities of various designs to be increased considerably. Not only was the performance of certain former GWR classes improved, but some LMS designs also had their maximum steaming rate nearly doubled. Other improvements in steam locomotive performance resulted from the development of Swindon's method of Controlled Road Testing, while it was a former GWR engineer who cured the perennial overheating problem with the centre big-ends on Gresley's Pacifics.

After nationalisation, British Railways embarked on the design and construction of a new series of standard steam locomotives. All the railway design offices were involved, each being given leadership with certain classes or covering specific features for all the locomotives. Most of the standard boilers built were based on the LMS versions of the Swindon designs, which Stanier had taken with him to Crewe. To supplement these designs, some existing classes continued to be built. As we have already seen, the construction of ten more Castles had taken place in 1946, and this was followed by a further thirty between 1948 and 1950. Following the completion of the last of these, no 7037, the locomotive was named 'Swindon' by HRH Princess Elizabeth during a visit to the works to mark the jubilee of the borough. Somewhat less expected, however,

was the appearance of two new classes of tank locomotive of GWR design after nationalisation. One of them was a lighter version of the 0-6-0 pannier tanks. Seventy of these 16XX class locomotives were built between 1949 and 1955, and their light axle loading resulted in two being transferred to the North of Scotland to work the former Highland Railway's Dornoch branch. Some of their larger brethren also travelled well off their parent system, being used as bankers on the Folkestone Harbour branch as well as the Lickey Incline. Others were bought by London Transport for use on engineers' trains when the third-rail current was switched off, and these out-lasted the use of steam locomotives on British Railways itself. The other new GWR design that appeared in 1949 was a great surprise. Pannier tanks were combined with *outside* cylinders and *outside* Walschaerts' valve gear. A very short wheelbase enabled them to traverse sharp curves, although they were in consequence somewhat unsteady at speed. Some, however, later passed into the ownership of the National Coal Board, where their ability to traverse the sharp curves of colliery yards was a considerable asset.

Even after the start of the diesel era on British Railways, the Western Region managed to pursue an individual path, arguing that they should develop diesel-hydraulic designs as an alternative to the diesel-electric locomotives being introduced on the other regions. Based on German experience, the new locomotives were much lighter, weighing the equivalent of two coaches less than a comparable diesel-electric design, such as the Class 40s, then known as the English Electric Type 4s. Several different diesel-hydraulic designs were produced, the most powerful being the D1000 class, which were all given a double-barrelled name, the first word of which was 'Western'. And just to rub it in, the first was named 'Western Enterprise'. Some of

John Ashman F.R.P.S.

37. The Western Region of British Railways used diesel-hydraulic locomotives extensively, the designs giving a significant weight advantage compared with contemporary diesel-electric classes. The most powerful of the diesel-hydraulics were the Class 52s, better known as the Westerns. The first of them, no D 1000 'Western Enterprise' is seen leaving High Wycombe, complete with cast name- and number-plates, as well as a *bas-relief* version of the BR lion and wheel emblem.

the complications of these designs can be seen by looking at the sectioned bogie from one of them which is exhibited in the National Railway Museum. In time high maintenance costs and poor reliability were to result in the scrapping of the diesel-hydraulics, a decision made possible because declining traffic on British Railways generally enabled them to redeploy sufficient diesel-electrics as replacements. The hydraulic designs, however, clearly showed the advan-

89

38. 'City of Truro' at Newbury in July 1957, working a Didcot to Southampton train. After being brought back from the Railway Museum at York, this was the route on which the locomotive was regularly used when not rostered for special excursions. One of the Hawksworth coaches, with its characteristic low-ended roof, is immediately behind the tender.

John Edgington

tages of low overall weights, and this feature was to be actively pursued in the design of the power cars of the InterCity 125s. In the late 1970s it was to be the Western Region that introduced 125mph running by these units in revenue service, making full use of the speed capabilities of Brunel's original main line to Bristol.

The Western Region took other opportunities to continue the Swindon tradition of naming

locomotives. In 1960 they managed to delay the construction of the last batch of Class 9F 2–10–0 freight locomotives so that to Swindon fell the honour of completing the last steam locomotive to be built for British Railways. It was duly named 'Evening Star' by Keith Grand, by then a member of the BTC, and instead of being finished in the standard black appeared in lined-green express-passenger livery complete with copper-capped chimney. Canton Sheds even rostered it for the 'Red Dragon' to Paddington before being told to stop. The standard livery adopted by British Railways for their express passenger steam locomotives was that used by the GWR, although there were differences in

39. At Drinnick Mill, in the midst of the Cornish china clay workings, the fireman of a St Blazey Pannier tank supervises taking water in August 1960 before cooking himself breakfast on the shovel.

detail. Metal plates on the smokebox replaced the numbers formerly painted on the buffer beam, but the use of cast metal numbers on the cab sides ensured that GWR locomotives retained their identity in the grand BR renumbering scheme. In the mid-1960s, Gerry Fiennes, then the General Manager, named several Class 47 diesels on the region as a reminder that the management was conscious of the past (but expected better in the future). In more recent times no 47500 has been named 'Great Western' and is used on Royal Trains and other prestige occasions. While sister locomotives elsewhere are named 'Great Eastern' and 'North Eastern', there are none today carrying plates that refer to the LNER or LMS. Chocolate and cream livery was also applied to BR Mk I coaches for certain expresses on the Western after the reorganisation of the BTC gave regions a greater degree of individual freedom.

It was in other fields of activity, however, that the outward appearances of the Great Western lived on with less change. The Hotels Executive never altered the name of the Great Western Royal Hotel at Paddington, and even today the letters GWR on the rear of the building above the station roof proclaim its origin across London. Although the Great Western operated the steamers on the Irish services, they were actually owned by the Fishguard & Rosslare Railways & Harbours. After 1948 this company was jointly owned by two nationalised organisations, the CIE in Eire, and the BTC in Britain, but that did not stop the ships continuing to sport GWR livery, including that company's coat of arms embossed on the bows. The 'St Patrick' in consequence stood out at Weymouth against the 'St Julien' and 'St Helier' which had received the Southern Railway's paint scheme that had been adopted as standard after nationalisation. The 'St Patrick's' design and facilities had benefited from two decades of progress compared with the other ships on the Weymouth-Channel Islands service, and many passengers deliberately chose it when booking their journeys.

Back in the 1930s, the Great Western Railway had presented their record-breaking locomotive 'City of Truro' to the railway museum at York, but with the increasing interest in steam locomotives as the modernisation plan progressed, it was duly recovered in 1957 by the Western Region, restored to working order at Swindon and used extensively on the Didcot & Southampton line as well as at the head of various special trains. It was retired once more in 1962 and joined the other exhibits at the new Great Western Railway Museum at Swindon, a joint enterprise between the Borough and the British Transport Commission. This museum was opened in June 1962 and in due course the ownership of most of the collection passed to the National Railway Museum under the terms of the 1968 Transport Act, although the building itself is now owned and operated by Thamesdown District Council, the successors of the Borough of Swindon. Not content with this considerable involvement in the official preservation scene, a large number of other GWR locomotives have subsequently been preserved, some being purchased directly from British Railways while others have been acquired from Dai Woodham's scrap yard at Barry. Examples of GWR rolling stock have also been preserved, including Special Saloons, and can be seen at many preservation sites throughout the country. There are thus many items of Great Western origin still to be found nearly forty years after the company ceased to exist, but these only represent one aspect of the continuation of the Great Western tradition to the present day.

5
God's Wonderful Railway

It is an extremely difficult task to sum up the Great Western Railway's achievements and traditions that now stretch back for 150 years. It has far more adherents, even today, than any other railway company in this country, as evinced by the numerous publications that have been devoted to its history and activities. Throughout the area it served it was respected and appreciated, and it is worth trying to determine the reasons for this widespread affection it succeeded in generating. It was to some extend founded on the fostering of the mutual financial interests of the railway and the industries it served. Direct statements were made by the company to the effect that it always endeavoured to purchase its requirements from organisations that used the GWR to transport their goods. Not for them was the public sector requirement, implied or otherwise, to accept the lowest tender submitted. It was perhaps only in South Wales where the GWR was not so universally popular, many doubtless seeing it as the English company that took over the Welsh railways at the grouping and thus presided over the economic troubles that followed during the inter-war years.

It is not possible to do justice to all the Great Western's many activities and achievements in the space available, but I would like to provide a brief series of vignettes that may help others to glimpse other facets of that organisation.

When Lloyd George died in 1945 he was buried in North Wales, and at the special request of the family, 'Dan', the Great Western's station horse at Criccieth, and well known to the Earl in his declining years, was used to draw the farm cart conveying the coffin to the grave beside the river Dwyfor. The local GWR carter led the simple procession with the Chief Horse Inspector in attendance, and both were subsequently thanked through the columns of the *Great Western Railway Magazine* for the part they played in the last journey of one of this country's twentieth century statesmen.

Towards the end of the steam era on the Western Region, the Kings and Castles with their high-superheat boilers were achieving some very fine performances on the main line to Bristol and South Wales. Normally on a railway there is an overall line speed limit in addition to the more restricted ones over curves, junctions etc, but for a brief period the Western Region specified no such limit, drivers being instructed to run at such speeds as were necessary to maintain the schedules specified in the timetables.

The following instruction used to appear in bold print inside the cover of every edition of the Great Western Railway's working timetables:

> Every care should be taken to avoid running over PACKS OF HOUNDS, which, during the Hunting Season, may cross the Line. All Railway employees are hereby enjoined to use every care consistent with a due regard being paid to the proper working of the Line and Trains.

Many of the guards on the principal expresses from the West of England used to sport floral sprays in their buttonholes during the spring and summer. The story goes that if a lady passenger admired the flowers, the guard would immediately take them out and make her a present of them. However, on his return to the guard's van he would replace them with another from the boxful provided by one of the local Cornish growers. Whether this is true or not I do not know, but the fact that it is still recounted is in itself illuminating and indicative of people's attitude to the Great Western and its staff.

So much of the Great Western's traditions and esprit de corps stemmed from their attitudes to people inside and outside the company. From the directors to a country goods porter, everyone had an important job to do. The homes of the members of the board were widely spread throughout the southern half of the country, and there always seemed to be one available locally to preside at any more-than-usually important event of a railway or commercial nature. The Chairman was no figurehead, and did not merely preside over board meetings while the chief officers ran the railway. When Sir Charles Hambro went to America on government business in 1944, Sir Edward Cadogan took over as Acting Chairman and promptly seized every

40. Viscount Portal, the last Chairman of the Great Western Railway, in relaxed mood on the footplate of the oil-burning 'Garth Hall' at Paddington in July 1946, a GWR wiper clutched in his right hand. More, perhaps, than any other single illustration, this photograph could be said to sum up the spirit of the Great Western Railway.

opportunity to gain first-hand information about the company's operations by visiting many of its main centres. At the final general meeting, Keith Grand commented that he thought the GWR was unique insomuch as the officers looked on the directors as their personal friends. It was significant too that at the end of the company's existence the directors firmly declined any compensation for loss of office, in contrast to the directors of the other three railways, where the shareholders proposed that they should be suitably rewarded (although the LNER motion was in fact defeated).

Staff welfare was a very important aspect of the Great Western Railway's managerial activities, but one of the most significant indicators of this is the sums of money advanced for staff housing schemes. As shown in Table 10, this amounted to nearly £¾ million in 1947, over three times the corresponding figure on the LNER, while the Southern's contribution came to well under £50,000. The LMS's general balance sheet did not itemise this particular heading.

As already mentioned, the physical assets of the four grouping companies, together with their operations, passed to the British Transport Commission at the beginning of 1948, leaving the old boards to convene their final general meetings in order to wind up their financial affairs. The usual statutory notices were sent out to shareholders, but it was the Great Western, alone, that included in this a reference to the undertaking and its staff. Viscount Portal concluded his brief report with the paragraph:

Apart from the formalities connected with the winding up of the Company, the Directors have fulfilled the only function left to them under the Transport Act 1947. The administration of the Undertaking is now in other hands but the Directors are confident that the staff will continue to maintain the standards of efficiency and courtesy which have always been the aim of the Company throughout its long period of existence.

At the meeting itself, the Chairman concluded his remarks to the shareholders by saying:

'To many of us the well-being of the railway has been part of our heritage, almost from boyhood days, and whatever changes the future may bring about we shall always remember with pride and affection the part we were privileged to play in dealing with the administration of the company's affairs, and the many friends we made amongst all classes of the community whilst acting in that capacity.'

In spite of all the technological, social and economic changes that have taken place over the years that have followed, it is sentiments like these that explain why memories of the Great Western and its traditions remain with us today.

Index

Index

Accidents 20, 34, 85
Acton Yard 13
Addison Road 36
Admiralty 19, 49
Aerial warfare 11, 13
Aircraft hazards 33–4, 47, 69
Aircraft Production, Ministry of 25
Air Raid Precautions 12, 16
Air raids 13, 14–15, Illus. 4
Air services 33, 54–6, 75
Alderney 72
'Alive' 24
Allison, George Illus. 11
Ambulance trains 24
Anderson, Sir Alan 54
Anderson air-raid shelters 12, 41
Anglo-Iranian Oil Co 65
Anti-aircraft guns 25, 41–2
Anzio 48
Approach Control System 87
Argentina 54
Associated Press 47
Augusta, U.S.S. 72
Austerity 38. *See also* Locomotives
'Automat' buffet-bar 66
Automatic Train Control 17, 85, Illus. 29
Automatic Warning System 87

Bananas 70
Barman, Christian 68
Barrage balloon equipment 25
Beeching Report 26, 67
Birkenhead 16, 81
Blackout 12–14, Illus. 3
Blenheim Palace 50

Block regulations 87
Bodleian Library 62
Boilers 20
Bomb damage 11, 12, 14–16, 28, 33–4, 71, Illus. 4, 5
Bombs 25, 43
Bridges 15–16
Bristol 12, 65, Illus. 5
British European Airways 75
British Railways 64, 65, 67, 82
British Railways in Peace and War 14, 54
British Transport Commission 65, 80, 81, 90, 92
Broccoli 38, Illus. 13
Buenos Aires 54
Buses 33, 72–3, 77
Butlin's Holiday Camps 68

Cadogan, Sir Edward 94
Canada 54
Canals 29, 49, 81
Canine hazards 94
Casualty coaches 24
Cattle 47, 75
Central Line (LPTB) 40, 67, Illus. 30
Channel Islands 46, 55
China 17
Churchill, Winston 16
CIE (Eire) 92
Clark, Kenneth 50
Coal
    Consumption 60, 87
    Cost 60
    Export 43–6, 70
    Household 38–9
    Quality 60
    Shortages 65, 70
    Trains 46

Cold weather 32, 60, 70
Condensing tenders 14
Cooper, George 16
Cornwall 38

D-Day 24, 28, 43–4, 49, 50
Departments of GWR
  Civil Engineering 66–9
  Goods & Traffic 50
  Stationery & Printing 70
Didcot, Newbury & Southampton Junction Railway 27–8
Diesel-electric locomotives 23, 65, 88–9
Diesel-hydraulic locomotives 88–90, Illus. 37
Diesel railcars 22, 25, 81, Illus. 9
Directors 11, 59, 84, 95
District Line (LPTB) 40
Dividends 78–9, 84
Docks 44–5, Illus. 19
Dow, George 56
Dunkirk 43, 47

Ealing Broadway 40
Eastleigh 17
Egyptian State Railways 19
Eisenhower, Gen. Dwight D. 24, 71
Electrification 60, 65
Elizabeth, Princess 88
Emergency (Railway Control) Order 11
Enquiry Office 30
Evacuation, civilian 31, 40–1, 72
Exeter 67

Festiniog Railway 68
Fiennes, G. 92
Fishguard & Rosslare Railways & Harbours 92
Flaman speed recorder 17
Floral buttonholes 94
Floral contretemps 38
Flying bombs 41–2
Fog 85
Food rationing 38, 52
Formica 66
French Railways (SNCF) 17, 22

Gas-turbine locomotives 65–6, Illus. 25
General Election (1945) 61
General Managers' Conference 11
George Cross 16
George VI, King 16
Glass roofs 12
Grand, Keith 57, 90, 94
Great Central Railway 18
Great Northern Railway 66
Gresley, Sir Nigel 66
'Great Way Round' 31

Hambro, Sir Charles 37, 57, 94
Harness competitions 73
Harrow collision 85–6
Highland Railway 88
Holiday Haunts 34
Home Guard 54, 57
Honeybourne 20
Horns, two-tone warning 22
Horses 16, 49, 50, 73, 81, 93
Horticultural shows 59
Hospital ships 46, 48, 72, Illus. 18
Hotels 50–2, 74–5, 81

Incendiary bombs 16
Inner Circle Line (LPTB) 16
Insulated vans 25
Interchange locomotive trials 87, Illus. 34
Iran 19
'Is Your Journey Really Necessary?' 31

Jersey and Guernsey Airways 55
Jones, C. M. Jenkin 46

Kennet & Avon Canal 29, 49

Leamington Spa 26
Leathers, Lord 20
Lee, Gen. John C. H. 71
Lickey Incline 88
Lighting 12–14, 20
Limestone 68
Livery 25, 91
Lloyd George, David 93
Locomotives
  American 19–20, 46
  'Austerity' 19–20
  Borrowed 16, 17, 18–9
  Britannia class 85
  Castle class 25, 65, 88, 93, Illus. 22, 35
  'City of Truro' 92, Illus. 38
  Collet 2251 class 17
  'Compton Castle' 62
  Dean Goods 17, Illus. 6
  'Evening Star' 90
  'Garth Hall' 65, Illus. 24, 40
  Hall class 22, 62, 65–6, Illus. 8
  'King Charles I' 15
  'King George VI' 54
  King class 25, 62, 87–8, 93
  Merchant Navy class (SR) 87
  Modified Hall Class 20, 62
  Pacific 68, 85, 88
  'Rhuddlan Castle' 65
  'Spitfire' Illus. 22
  Stroudley Terriers 37
  'Swindon' 88

Tank 14, 60, 88, Illus. 36, 39
'Tiny' 15
'Viscount Portal' 62
War Department 17–19
16XX series 88
28XX series 20, 87
39XX series 65
41XX series 94
48XX series 65
70XX series 62–3
94XX series 64
Locomotive wheel arrangements
  0–6–0 17, 22, 63–4
  0–6–0 (LMS, LNER) 17
  0–6–0T 64
  0–6–0T (USA) 20
  2–8–0 19–20, 29, 46, 65, Illus. 7
  2–8–0 (LMS) 18–19
  2–8–0 (WD) 18
  2–8–2T 22
  2–10–0 90
  4–4–2T (SR) 19
  4–6–0 (SR) 19
London Midland & Scottish Railway 11, 12, 18–20, 23–4, 26, 29, 39, 49
London & North Eastern Railway 19, 20, 22–3, 38, 40, 46, 69
London Passenger Transport Board 67, 75, 80
London & South Western Railway 26, 27

McAlpine (Sir Robert) & Sons 29
Maidenhead Illus. 14
Mails 35, 46, 70, 72
Malvern College 50
Manor House Hotel 75
Margam 69
Matthews, Sir Ronald 20
Metropolitan Vickers 65
Midland Railway 17
Milne, Sir James 11, 42
Milton Keynes 67
Minesweepers 47
Mobile canteens 52, 53
Mobile military HQ 24–5
Montgomery, General B. 24–5
Morrison air-raid shelters 41
Munition factories 35–6
Museums 50, 65, 89, 92

Nameboards, station 33
Naming policy 17
Narrow-gauge lines 70
National Coal Board 88
National Fire Service 57
National Gallery 50
Nationalisation 22, 80, 81–4, 85

National Savings 59
National Union of Railwaymen 75
Newton Abbot 14–15, Illus. 4
Next Station 68, 74–5
Nominated loading 38
North Eastern Railway 17

Ocean liners 72
Oil firing 65, Illus. 24
Oil wharves 22
Operation 'Overlord' 44
Ottoman Railway 17
Owen, Mary 47
Oxford 24, 26, 29, 60, 62
Oxford City Council 62
Oxford University 62

Paddington 13, 14, 30, 42, 54, 67
Parcels 22, 49
Passenger trains 32–3
Pears, Charles 47
Penzance 32
Peterborough 67
Photography 34, 47
Piccadilly Line (LPTB) 11
Pile, Gen. Sir Frederick 57
Pillboxes 29
Plymouth 12, 26
Points operation 28
Portal, Viscount 94–5, Illus. 40. See also Locomotives
Posters 12, 31, Illus. 1
Preservation of railways 69, 92
Prisoners of War 44

'Q' campaign 38

Rabbits 38–9
Radio communications 29–30
Railway Control Agreement 80
Railway Executive Committee 31, Illus. 1
Railway Gazette 38
Railway Technical Committee 11
'Rapier' 25
Reading 27
Renown, H.M.S. 72
Reservation of seats 34, Illus. 1
Restaurant cars 32, 50, 70, Illus. 1, 3, 28
Road vehicles 49–50, 72–3
Robinson, J. G. 18
Royal trains 62, 72, 92
Ryan, Col. 20

Shareholders 68, 78, 84, 95
Shipping services 46
Ships
  Lakehurst (US) 46

Mew 47
Roebuck 47, 72
St Andrew 46, 72
St David 47, 48, 71, 72
St Helier 46, 47, 49, 72, 92
St Julien 49, 72, 92
Sambur 47, 72
Shunting 19, 20, 23, 64, 73, 81
Signalling 28, 29, 69, 85, 87, Illus. 36
'Siphon G' vans 24
Slate 61
Sleepers 29
Sleeping coaches 25, 32, 66
Slip carriages 32
Smith, Simon Rocksborough 67
Snow hazards 60
Southern Railway 12, 19, 24, 26, 27, 28, 40, 55
Spanish Civil War 11
Speed restrictions 87, 93
Spitfire funds 59
'Square Deal' campaign 78
Staff
    Calendar 73
    Canteens 54, 75
    Female 33, 57
    Gallantry awards 47
    Hostels 54, 59
    Housing 81, 94
    Statistics 57, 81
    War casualties 59
    Welfare 94
Staines Moor 27
Stations 35
Steam pressure 62
Stevenage 67
Superheating 63, 64, 87, 93
Switzerland 65

Tank traps 28
Taunton 29, 39
Tenders, locomotive 62

Tenders, ocean liner 49, 72
Thamesdown District Council 92
Thomas, David St John 67
Thompson, Edward 20
Tickets
    Cheap day 34, 70
    Monthly return 70
    Sailing 72
    Season 36
Timekeeping 32–3
Tracks 14, 26–30, 34, 66–8, 85
Trains
    'Bristolian' 31
    'Cheltenham Flyer' 31
    'Cornish Riviera' 25
    'Coronation' (LNER) 31
    'Torbay Express' 25
Travelling Post Office 70
Troopships 47
Truman, President Harry S 72
Tugs 47
Tunna, Norman 16
Turkey 19

United Nations 17

Vacuum brakes 70
Vale of Rheidol line 70
Vienna 66
Volunteer labour 38

Wagons 25, 38, 39–40, 61
Walschaerts' valve gear 88
War Department locomotives 17
War Transport, Ministry of 19, 38, 42, 49
Waters, G. O. 55
Westinghouse brakes 17
Weston, Clevedon and Portishead Railway 36–7
Whittle, Sir Geoffrey 65
Woodham, Dai 92
World War I 11, 17–19